GW00771960

Training Dogs for Protection Work

Training Dogs for Protection Work

FRED MANDILK MA
and
MARV GANGLOFF

J. A. Allen
LONDON

First published in Great Britain 1999
Reprinted 2006
Reprinted 2008

ISBN 978-0-85131-736 -6

J.A. Allen
Clerkenwell House
Clerkenwell Green
London EC1R 0HT

J.A. Allen is an imprint of Robert Hale Limited

www.halebooks.com

British Library Cataloguing in Publication Data
A catalogue record for this book is available from the British Library

Photographs by Fred and Olivia Mandilk and Ken Moberg
Photograph on page 18 by kind permission of the Imperial War Museum; photograph on page 150 by kind permission of the Metropolitan Police Service, Directorate of Public Affairs and Internal Communication.
Line drawings by Lil Gangloff

Printed in China and arranged by New Era Printing Co Ltd, Hong Kong

Contents

List of Photographs

Foreword

Professional dog training being an inexact science, it has always been my profound belief that, as a subject, it is one of the least likely to be conveyed by the written word. Although it is possible to give general guidance it must always be remembered that each dog is an individual; a method of training that suits the temperament, previous background and ability of one may not prove successful with another, it could even have an adverse effect which in certain cases would be irreversible.

With these thoughts in mind, plus the added prevalence of psycho babble and 'new thinking' which has recently permeated the whole dog training scene, I commenced to read the page proofs of Fred Mandilk's and Marv Ganglov's book mainly devoted to that controversial branch of our subject: the training of the protection dog.

To my surprise and pleasure I found the book to be orthodox in its approach with a down-to-earth attitude which not only raised my spirits but also renewed my faith in the future of dog training. I feel sure that as an introduction to this type of work it will be of immense help to the beginner and possibly give some new avenues of thought to the initiated.

The authors, who train for 35 police departments in the USA, explain the use of equipment and methods which may be unfamiliar to the reader and, although it has to be said that The British Institute of Professional Dog Trainers do not advocate the use of any particular training aid or method (our only criterion is that the methods and equipment used are mentally and physically humane), after reading the book I have no reason to doubt that, if used correctly, these methods would not constitute a breach of that criterion.

Tom Buckley,
General Secretary, British Institute of Professional Dog Trainers.

Publisher's Note

This book is aimed at readers who have a serious interest in training and handling working protection dogs. Such activities are not to be undertaken lightly, or by inexperienced people, and the publisher strongly recommends that the owners and handlers of such dogs seek expert advice from a member of the British Institute of Professional Dog Trainers (or their own nation's official organization) before embarking upon practical training. British owners are also advised to make themselves fully familiar with the provisions and requirements of *The Dangerous Dogs Act* and the *Guard Dog Act*.

Whilst the procedures and practices outlined in this book are based upon the extensive experience of expert authors, neither the authors nor the publisher will accept liability for any incident arising out of the training or handling of protection dogs.

Authors' Note

The training system described in this book is fundamentally based upon a psychological understanding of, and respect for, the working dog. We state repeatedly that correct training is based upon reward reinforcement and that correction, in any form, should be kept to a minimum. However, we recognize that some of the equipment and procedures described may be unfamiliar to, or misunderstood by, certain readers, and we therefore feel it appropriate to clarify these issues as follows.

Collars

The work describes three collars: two for training and one for easy use. The latter is the 'fur-saver' collar which is basically a large-ringed 'choke' chain. Most novice working dogs will not feel a correction from this collar. The 'protection' collar is used during bite training. This collar is a 1½–2 inch (4–5 cm) wide leather collar worn loosely so that the dog uses his lower neck muscles when pulling toward the decoy. The 'correction' collar is the 'pinch' collar. This collar is used for training purposes with nearly all working dogs, no matter what their level of training. Proper training does not use the collar to punish a dog into behaving as desired, but to correct the dog (negative reinforcement) to perform a behaviour already learned (through the early use of positive reinforcement, toy or food reward). Positive reinforcement alone works consistently with dogs handler-raised from five weeks old until the dog reaches early maturity (fourteen to eighteen months). At this age the good working dog becomes hard-headed, and thus positive reinforcement becomes unpredictable in new and unusual environments.

Why wouldn't some other collar work? The working dog of good genetic background has such high drives that he simply would not feel anything less than a pinch collar. Indeed, we often see dogs slated for police departments because they are so hard-headed that the pinch collar is useless. Handlers of such dogs resort to the electric shock collar in order to get compliance in the 'out' and other forms of obedience. Such dogs generally learn to comply for only weeks at a time, then their previous mental attitude of hard-headedness returns, along with the electric collar. The electric collar is only for the extreme dog.

The Forced Retrieve

Teaching the Schutzhund forced retrieve often causes novice trainers and handlers to look askance at the entire training programme. It is the first and only time that the handler may cause genuine and deep confusion in the dog. Yet, this is temporary and it counters the dog's maturation process that begins to challenge the handler at around the age of fourteen to eighteen months.

Very few working calibre dogs will hold and keep an object like a dumb-bell unless they are taught to do so. The dog's level of judgment is not generally high enough to learn the procedure through toy or food reinforcement (we are not saying that it is impossible, only unlikely). As with all training, the secret is trainer patience without urgency or anxiety. As for most training, the basic procedure takes three or four sessions before understanding begins to occur. It certainly helps if the dog already knows the 'take' command before beginning the procedure. About four to five weeks before beginning the procedure, we begin giving the 'take' command whilst holding the toy and whilst pointing at it on the ground. Once he takes the toy, we throw a second toy for reinforcement. The result is that the dog has a notion of the 'take' command. This reduces the compulsive element in teaching the dog merely to retain the dumb-bell.

The psychological purpose of the forced retrieve is to mitigate the maturing novice dog's increased aggressiveness toward the handler. The practical purpose is to teach the dog that he must take and hold those items that the handler selects.

Introduction

However, ask, please, the domestic animals, and they will instruct you;
Also the winged creatures of the heavens, and they will tell you.
Or show your concern to the earth, and it will instruct you;
And the fishes of the sea will declare it to you.
Who among all these does not well know
That the hand of Jehovah itself has done this,
In whose hand is the soul of everyone alive and the spirit of all flesh of man?

Job, speaking to his accusers, asserting, among many things,
that even domestic animals teach us. Job 12:7-10

The purpose of this handbook is to provide fundamental information to the new working dog handler. It offers guidelines, examines behavioural expectations of the dog and suggests appropriate training attitudes for the role of handler. Within these pages, we will define training terms and show how understanding your dog's shifts in protection phases (between the two drives of prey and defence) help determine the quality of training. Beginning with the puppy and continuing through adulthood, we will show the various strategies and techniques for obedience, tracking and protection.

A common problem with new handlers of adult working dogs, especially novice police handlers, is the lack of knowledge concerning the training the dog receives before he enters the department or home. Trainers do their best to fit the dog with the handler but, more often than not, it is the dog who does most of the adjusting. We feel that the more the handler knows about the three areas of training (tracking, obedience and protection) the less mysterious and confusing they appear, and the more likely it is that costly mistakes will not occur.

Civilian handlers have other problems as well. It is a sad observation that most trainers and sleeve helpers either fail to study, or fail to continue studying, dog learning theory. Thus, many inexperienced handlers have little choice but to work with a novice sleeve helper. This combination produces a situation that at best (given a helper with raw talent), provides on-the-job helper education through making training mistakes. This trial and error method of teaching either slows, stops or ruins even a good dog's progress or attitude. In the worse scenario, helpers who refuse to learn from their own track record of ruined dogs continue to do so as unsuspecting handlers flow in and out of the dog club.

Often, competent handlers who know what to look for in a trainer learn by that most difficult, but thorough of methods: personal experience. As new and unschooled handlers they unknowingly watched their dogs trained wrongly, but sometimes understood the situation far too late. Over time, the competent handler learned how to spot the improper trainer: by the methods used. Poor training methods show little respect for the handler, but especially little for the dog. More concisely, poor training methods fail to *learn from the dog*. This handbook will alert the new and

Early tracking training.

inexperienced handler of the need to avoid the untrained sleeve helper – or, at least, it will provide the means of articulating requests that trainers and helpers follow training directions and theories.

Our goal is to produce a handbook that will be helpful to all forms of protection dog training (police, military and civilian) for we teach understanding of the dog, rather than the enhancement of handler and trainer ego through the sterile method of behaviourism. Understanding the training and psychology of these powerful animals produces more than a mere working dog or a glorified pet; it produces an important addition to our human family. A family member who will instruct us exactly how to teach dog training, and much more. This therefore, is a form of understanding that crosses political, cultural and national boundaries.

CHAPTER ONE
Handler-Dog Relationships

> It is a great compliment to man, that when he does find the soul of anything, and uses it well, how wonderful is the response! It may be said, that, as a whole, this happy state has, to a great extent, been reached in regard to the dog, which...is so closely in touch with the mind of his master, and we are beginning to perceive that many characteristics which we have hitherto considered as belonging exclusively to human beings, and far above the animals, are really as much within the possession of our dogs as of ourselves.
>
> E.H. Richardson, 1920

Perhaps the new or inexperienced working dog handler may not fully comprehend the feeling Richardson so eloquently expresses. This is regrettable, since the passage offers a fine rationale for training the working dog. If this is applies to you, cheer up, for you may in due course achieve an unusual state of communion with that alien species which we take for granted as 'the dog'. However, communication at this level takes time and technique. Communication, as we define the term, is not marvellous but mindless circus acts that impress the audience and bolster the handler's ego. Communication with the *working* dog is what Richardson writes about; it is the contact and understanding between a human and his dog. Mundane in words, but beautiful if you are lucky enough to truly experience the feeling.

Some may ask, 'Why own a working dog?' Or, getting closer to the substance of the working protection dog, 'Why teach your dog protection, tracking and obedience?' There are many valid and invalid reasons for training and owning a working dog.

Some people, or professions, require protection. Police departments purchase dogs for officers; military organizations use dogs for guarding facilities; citizens often need dogs to guard homes and family.

From the dog's point of view, there are some breeds that need to work; indeed, it's their very reason for existence. Without training, such high-powered animals will cost the owner hundreds, if not thousands of pounds in property destroyed through sheer boredom. Therefore, if you have such a dog and you're trying to work out what to do with him, observe a Schutzhund trainer in action. A very good training course will improve the dog's character and make him a joy around the house. These animals not only enjoy working – they will teach a competent handler how to teach them! Furthermore, good teaching will soon establish a bond between dog and handler. Each will know what to expect from the other. This is true even if the dog cannot take part in trials because of poor protection, obedience, or tracking skills. A correctly trained protection dog will not become 'savage' or 'mean', but will remain a dog with self-confidence, based upon the experience of training.

Schutzhund training is not simply teaching a dog to bite an attacker. The purpose of the three areas in Schutzhund training (tracking, obedience, and protection) is to guide the dog's instincts in a way that will benefit his owner. This is how we define the 'working dog'. In the event that the dog is unable to pass the Schutzhund test or a police trial, despite the competent handler's best efforts, the handler still passes the more important test of responsible dog ownership. Such an owner obtains a dog and trains him until the dog shows that he is unable to keep his confidence amidst the stresses of training, yet the team tightness is still apparent to any observer. On the other hand, the lucky and skilful handler may find that he has the right combination of dog and training to pass the test.

The process of teaching a dog is also beneficial to the handler. In the high-tech world of superficial nonsense, the team spirit of a handler and dog provide more than relief, being something close to the sacred communication between two species that was once common on family farms. It is only after innumerable hours of solid training that handler and dog reach this point of teamwork. This is not to say that they achieve perfection, but rather a truly mutual understanding.

In today's society, a properly trained protection dog can be more than useful. Despite our 'freedom', we often live with violence. Robberies, burglaries, and physical assault are common almost everywhere. This, alone, is a reason to have a dog trained to help if you or your family need assistance. It is far better to have a trained and trusted protection dog than an untrained and untested dog who runs away from a determined assault, or attacks an innocent party.

So, there are many positive reasons for training dogs – were you expecting to hear differently in a book about dogs? Yet, there are also some very good reasons for not owning a dog. While dogs are an incredible source of affection, they are also excessively egocentric. Many trainers compare the adult dog with the two-year-old child. Get the picture? Therefore, owning and training a perpetual two-year-old is a commitment to devote time every day to greet, talk to and teach the dog, and provide care. If this is not possible, then working dog ownership is not for you.

Commitment to Training

The handler must teach the working dog to maintain and increase self-confidence. Working dogs, like children, are not trained for circus-like control or to become less bothersome. Rather, superior training provides a predictable reaction to situations that avoids discomfort or injury to the dog and produces a dog with an attitude that benefits the handler and the family. Ideally, with respectful training, the dog's self-confidence matures and eventually replaces a puppyhood mentality based upon companionship. The mature dog displays boldness and alertness toward the surrounding environment.

Thoughtful training contributes to producing an alert dog as opposed to a submissive dog. The first step of formal training is to teach the dog how to learn. This means that he learns to respond to correction out of choice, not submission. The superior trainer views disobedience not as a revolt, but merely as an inappropriate behaviour that produces for the dog something negative, or a lack of something positive.

So how do we teach the dog how to learn? When beginning a new behaviour routine with a novice adult dog, every minor correction producing the desired response is immediately rewarded. The reward may be simply reaching down and giving a soft pat on the side whilst saying, 'that's it'.

For example, when teaching the dog to walk to heel, the handler lightly corrects the forging adult dog with the training collar. Upon compliance, the handler immediately reaches down (while still in motion) to stroke the dog lightly, combining this action with short but enthusiastic verbal praise. (An alternative is to throw the chase toy, the most important training tool.)

The training tool.

Once the dog knows a routine, or several training routines, training is a game to him, in which he receives positive reinforcement such as a ball or verbal praise. When the dog is having fun, the handler enjoys the work as well – and training sessions may be long.

However, when you are introducing a new behaviour, or working on an unmastered behaviour, be sure to keep the training time short – only a minute or so – and then launch into a mastered routine. The rule is: when pressure is on the dog to learn a new behaviour, keep it short. You may work on a new routine three or four times a day, but keep each unmastered segment of the session within a few minutes. As the dog catches on, increase the time element. With short training periods, fatigue and confusion – and even possible distrust – become less of a factor.

When introducing a new routine, it is important to remember to allow all the other mastered behaviours to go back to pre-school level. This means not demanding perfect performances, but allowing the dog to be a little sloppy, thus taking the pressure away. When he is carrying out the new behavioural routine satisfactorily, you can easily clean up the pre-school sloppiness in the other areas. This will take very little time, since he knows what is expected. This procedure effectively avoids combining the pressure from the new behaviour with the unnecessary pressure of strictly enforced mastered behaviours.

For example, when introducing the send away, the dog enters a state of confusion as to what the handler wants. After a few minutes of working on the send away, the dog is put through the mastered heeling routine. Here we take away nearly all negative correction (pressure) and apply mostly rewards (ball, toy throwing or jute stick) for correct behaviour. The trainer uses this reward method for even the slightest correct behaviour, such as heeling in position for even two or three feet. The next reward comes after the correct right turn. Thus the mastered routine turns into a major play session; this produces a happy team.

The typical mistake committed by novice trainers is the erroneous belief that the new behaviour should be the only behaviour worked on during training. This is not the case. As pointed out above, it is desirable to work on a few mastered behaviours and just one new behaviour during the training session. The dog then views the mastered behaviours with confidence, thereby lessening the confusion that accompanies the introduction of a new behaviour.

It is important to realize that the confusion produced by teaching new behaviours tears down the team spirit until such time as the dog understands. The handler must watch and read the dog closely to note when the dog is at the point of understanding. With understanding comes sterner corrections, that temporarily remove the playful edge from the dog. With one dog, the handler knows that he is on the correct mental track when he returns with his toy giving eye contact for the final twenty yards. The handler always get the feeling that the dog is saying 'Now I get it!' On the other hand, when he does not fully understand, he concentrates on the toy in his mouth while avoiding eye contact during his return. At the point of understanding, the high-powered working dog needs a somewhat stern correction when he begins to lark about – which he almost certainly will do because the play method is one of the first attitudes he learned!

There is a curious distinction between a dog carrying out a certain behaviour correctly and *understanding* the behaviour. Through training, the dog may do what is required, but not understand what he is doing – he is therefore not thinking. Such a dog lacks full self-confidence. This is the outcome of trained animal shows and obedience trials where thinking is undesirable. You will see in Chapter 2 that we choose the alert and bold pup who is full of energy. We do not want to suppress these traits, but to guide them. Using the play method helps to reach this point of understanding, causing a return of self-confident alertness in both body language and demeanour, thereby embellishing the original traits with learning. When this happens across all training parameters, we have a true working dog; one who is capable of independent thinking.

Good training will provide a working dog who happily puts up with restraint just for the sake of being near the handler. The happy working dog does not want 'freedom' to roam the countryside or city block on his own, but only to be with his handler. Such a dog becomes excited when training time approaches and the handler appears; excitement increases with the slipping on of the tracking harness, or as the obedience leash hooks onto the training collar. On sleeve days the excitement may begin several miles from the training grounds. These not-so-subtle clues point to correct training and a happy dog.

Training guides the dog from being one who wants to roam, distracted by everything around him, unable to pay any attention to his handler, to one quite alert to his handler *and* his environment. When handler understanding and kindness enter the training picture, the dog's self-confidence and trust increase further. Importantly, with the training techniques described, the handler and dog will have an enjoyable experience, and will look forward with positive anticipation to the next training session.

Attention on handler, not distracted by surroundings.

On the other hand, bad or incompetent handling has the opposite effect upon both dog and handler. People with angry personalities or those who have large and uncontrolled egos should not work dogs, for here there is no trust and without trust there can be no team. The dog learns, alongside other behaviours, the psychological disposition of the handler at any given moment. The dog forced to work with a handler who exhibits mood swings becomes unstable himself. Psychological instability equates to lack of self-control, and lack of self-control always produces a dog out of control. Self-control is important within any training phase since, without it, confusion will grow from irrational behaviour. The end result is training delays, or worse. Again, patience and understanding are all-important in dog training, for no dog works so well as for the handler with self-control and maturity.

To avoid misunderstanding, this is a good point at which to define terms. When good trainers speak of 'understanding' the dog, or showing the dog 'kindness', they are not communicating some form of slushy sentiment, but viewing the world through the eyes of the dog. The handler must study canine psychology and love working dogs without ascribing to them human psychology or motivation. Many German dog clubs have the motto: *Wer Hunde Lehren will, muss sie versteh'n muss selbst durch Hundeargen seh'n Er neige liebevoll zum Hund sich hin und prufe Hunde Herz und Sinn.*[1]

This can be translated as: 'The competent handler must view the world through the dog's eyes, combining love with understanding of the canine's soul and mind'. Once the handler can, more often than not, guess correctly what is going on inside the mind of his dog, he is not only viewing the world in general through his dog, but viewing himself as well. Such perception provides invaluable feedback during training.

The final triumph of the dog/handler team is that they become paired for life. As the dog ages and continues to work with the same knowledgeable trainer, he increases in self-confidence and gains in willingness to please. With the passage of time, he learns to 'read' his handler! Therefore, assuming the dog has a good genetic working background, combined with proper training methods, he becomes more knowledgeable and teachable. This situation is achieved only by the handler who loves teaching the dog and has the ability to do so.

Let us consider briefly this special relationship between the working dog and the handler. The basis for this interaction is the pack mentality. Frequent companionship between the handler and the dog, especially where aggression occurs (rag or sleeve work), builds the social standards of the pack in the mind of the dog. Since the mother lays the groundwork for social hierarchy, it is important

[1] Wimhurst 1967, page 194.

to select a pup from a normal litter. Boosted by obedience and tracking work, the dog's self-confidence will grow, along with a natural submissiveness (pack/social drive) to his handler. The core of every dog and handler team consists of this natural submissiveness, which occurs almost spontaneously as a consequence of working and learning together. The novice handler oversteps the boundary of natural submissiveness because of either conscious or unconscious fears of his dog. Such a handler views many misbehaviours as acts of rebellion and ends up over-reacting; virtually attacking the dog with severe forms of over-correction.

Yet, even the most misunderstood dog may find what he needs in his handler through bite training. In a way which is similar to the young wolf gaining confidence through participating with the pack in bringing down game, so self confidence increases in dogs with bite work. However, controlling the dog reduces confidence. This also occurs in the wolf pack, when the alpha pair (pack leaders) command pack members to back-off. Therefore, many trainers feel that bite work reduces the depression caused by compulsive obedience. However, it should be borne in mind that the three areas of training influence one another and, for this reason, we recommend that the dog receives compulsive obedience training during defence bite work, not before. The theory behind this choice of training progression is that if the dog is biting well with defence pressure, then added pressure with dumb-bell training may not harm the bite. However, if the dog is not biting with defence pressure, compulsive dumb-bell work may cause confusion because of the unusual treatment from the handler. Any behavioural analysis must always include consideration of what is happening in the other two areas of training.

The Working Dog and Competition

Beside anger, there are other sources of ego dysfunction, some institutionalized, that lead to a confused dog. As long as we adhere to the received fundamentals of Schutzhund training, there will be serious drawbacks. Observation of competitive dog trials, both

Schutzhund and police, especially at the higher levels, show that some apparent dog experts only enjoy their dog when he responds like a machine, thereby increasing their ego satisfaction. They are unable to study the psychology of their charges effectively. We note the programmed 'protection' dog who will only hold and bark at the helper in the blind, but not at the judge standing a few feet outside the blind. There is often incomplete training of competitive dogs which produces the 'sleeve happy' dog, making the dog useless in the world of violent reality and a mockery of the term 'working dog'. At this point, competitive trials become artificial, far removed from the definition of 'working dog'. In a real-life situation, such a dog becomes confused and will not hold the attacker since he is not in the blind, or may not bite him because he is not wearing a sleeve. The relatively new competitive standards of training teach these dogs *not* to think.

Because of our cultural orientation that embraces competition, we note an increase in highly competitive Schutzhund trials. Instead of simply passing the test of Schutzhund as in yesteryear, handlers now compete for the highest points, trophies, and so on. Building upon the competitive nature of the majority of modern handlers, Schutzhund clubs reduce themselves to a 'sport' mentality. Indeed, there is a movement in the United States to include protection trials in the Olympics.

Once points and prestige become overriding concerns, team spirit suffers as the dog becomes compelled to perform at the machine level. As mentioned above, such competition dogs are no longer 'working dogs'. These dogs become kennelled during non-training hours because their handlers feel that the dog must depend upon only one person for everything. The dog does not patrol the home, run in the yard, or play with the children, but sits in a kennel awaiting a chance to perform as an extension of human ego. The paradox here is that Schutzhund as a test is intended for breeding purposes. That is, the function of Schutzhund is to produce and continue excellent genetic traits of only those dogs who pass the test. These dogs are allowed to contribute to the gene pool for *working dogs*, not the entirely different class known as sport dogs. Helen Sherlock warns us that:

> Merely to use the dog as an extension of man's ego satisfaction, of his desire for more efficient machinery for often very selfish and shortsighted goals, implies the use of force and gruelling routine to elicit a specific response. This can only result in the destruction of the balance and richness of the dog's potential and man's loss of another link with his own sources of creativity....The dog becomes the owner's self-extension, to some degree.[2]

Professional Trainers

Handlers must study their dogs. The buzz word for this study today is 'reading' the dog. This term appears almost mystical to both old-timers and novices alike. The uncertainty amongst old-time trainers is evident as one rarely finds two trainers who will read a dog identically. Meanwhile, the trusting handler goes along for the ride. Hopefully, after reading this book, the new handler will come away with a foundation of knowledge leading to self-reflection and the ability to generate solid questions before, during and after the training session. The knowledgeable handler fully understands that there is only one 'trainer', – himself, for it is the handler who must bear all responsibility (and the blame as well) when training goes awry.

Care and Rapport

It is a sad commentary on modern culture's lack of connection with domestic animals that we feel compelled to talk about meeting the basic needs of the dog. First, most trainers believe that only the handler should provide care for the dog. Further, handlers always care for their dog's needs before their own. For example, provide your dog with a small amount of water after a workout before attending to your own needs. If you satisfy your own comfort first, you may forget the dog's. The same is true for feeding. If the handler comes home late, looking forward to that fresh, hot pizza, the needs of the dog are still attended to first, not resentfully, but out of respect.

[2] Little, Brown 1978, page xii.

In order to maintain the team, only the handler should work the dog. If the handler has to go on an overnight trip without the dog, and must therefore place him in a kennel, then an arrangement must be made to ensure that the dog receives light exercise twice a day, with no bite work or obedience practice. This avoids inconsistent demands upon the dog and maintains handler/dog rapport.

Handler/dog rapport is an issue of fundamental importance. In domestic dogs the pack rapport trait tends to include all human beings. With training, and with a modified home environment where only the handler cares for the dog, this trait shrinks to the size of the handler/dog team.

The foundation of rapport is praise. For most dogs, physical and verbal praise must be substantial during training. Many dog handlers well understand the value of physical praise. However, we note many methods. Some handlers rarely make contact beyond the head region; others pound and slap their dogs; some stroke a dog like a cat; a few stroke only the tips of the hair. Most of these methods are acceptable to the dog, although some dogs do not like slaps or heavy pounding. Most importantly, dogs need and enjoy verbal praise even more than physical praise. Verbal praise is possible whenever the dog is within hearing range. In all phases of training, such praise is the most important guiding aspect to the dog – so use plenty.

Related to physical reinforcement is the act of massage. After a heavy workout, knowledgeable trainers provide their dogs with a simple massage. A soothing massage begins in the neck area, continuing down to the toes, the idea being to dispel any physical soreness.

Behavioural Psychology

Let us briefly enter the academic realm of behavioural psychology. The effective use of praise is a classical form of conditioning. When the dog hears a word that he identifies (from past experience) with a toy, he will respond both consciously and unconsciously. Over time, he will associate both the praise words and the toy with his current behaviour. For instance, if we reward the dog for current behaviour by combining a thrown toy with the words 'good boy', the phrase will be associated with the toy (prey) which gives a pleasurable response, such as salivating or anticipating a hunt. This pleasurable response will eventually occur as a consequence of the associated phrase, even if the toy doesn't appear. This is how verbal praise becomes possible. Physical touch may be added or substituted for this type of conditioning.

There is another form of conditioning that behaviourists call 'operant'. This occurs when the dog does something on the field because he wants the reward. Thus, if the dog believes that there may be a toy in the blind, he will run to the blind: he is 'operating' on the environment to get the reward.

'Shaping' is a behavioural term of major significance in training. For example, using the blind and toy training situation just cited, we can shape the dog to run happily to the blind. The first step is to sit the dog a short distance from the blind and place the toy near the blind. Then, with the toy in plain sight, the dog is given the 'search' command. He runs a few feet and gets the toy. The next session finds the dog a little further back. The following session, after a few runs with the toy in sight, it is placed behind the blind. The dog will go to the blind because he thinks the out-of-sight toy must be there. This is the process of 'shaping', and it starts during puppy training! The creative use of the shaping process is the foundation of the training art.

After analysing an entire routine, consider how you can break it down into small steps, applying shaping for each step. For each step, consider when to give the reinforcer, or toy. Upon the conclusion of the successful shaping of steps, put it all together. In the blind search example, each training step occurred by increasing the distance from the blind. The next step is to approach the blind (the dog in 'stay') as usual, but this time keep the toy instead of leaving it in the blind. Return to the dog and send him for the toy that is not there. Once he is in the blind, call him and excitingly show him the toy in your hand. Upon his return, throw the toy behind you. On the next try, put the toy in the blind as he expects. Sending him to the blind and then calling him back is called 'chaining': you have chained two behaviours together (the 'search' and the 'come'), leading to a new behaviour.

In the beginning, to keep motivation high, the blind search is pretty much like the old shell trick. The dog doesn't know whether the toy is in the blind or not but, when called, he knows that you have the toy. The point here is that the difficult part of training is simply discovering how to break a routine down into small, shapable behaviours that you can reinforce and then connect. Good trainers use a lot of imagination! This is why, even if you find two trainers who read a dog identically, they may have different shaping methods to reach the same goal.

Discipline

Corrective discipline (punishment) is becoming more difficult in the current social state of 'abusism'. When in public, correct the dog with the knowledge that someone may misunderstand your behaviour and call the police, who are much more likely than ever before to act. In consequence, dog discipline is now about as mystical as the protection phase of training.

Even the phrases used for identifying dog gear are coming under attack. Items such as 'choke' chains or 'pinch' collars are two tools that confirm in some minds the idea that training abuses dogs. People who are uninformed about high-powered dogs tend to associate the working dog with the mild and handler-sensitive Golden Retriever. Many young working dogs may not respond to a command without an accompanying pinch collar correction. During training, the command itself guides the dog to do something, and the correction reminds him that he must comply. Thus, in correct training, the dog does not respond to force, but to his handler's direction.

While training collar discipline is always a part of the working dog culture, there is an important dramatic element that may help preclude its use. The best trainers often apply discipline by simply using a lot of drama. Discipline is a natural facet of life. Dogs first experience discipline from their mother; trainers build from this point. The trainer must approach discipline with a businesslike attitude and with an underlying sense of humour. Discipline is more or less play-acting, but the dog must only see that you are serious. In short, discipline requires drama in the form of using fake threats, good timing and, in some cases, passage of time.

Disciplining a dog may bring up questions of the dog's feelings. Do dogs have feelings? Dog owners and many psychologists state that they do indeed. Furthermore, they are incapable of hiding their feelings, which become apparent in body posture, movement, and facial expressions. The dog's body language is thus very similar to our own, making the dog the ideal companion. Indeed, the feelings and body language that we and dogs have in common cement the dog/human 'pack'. Dogs, like people, are social, or 'pack' animals. Since both groups are social, dogs easily maintain the pack instinct in the company of people *because they believe they understand us*. This pack allegiance is an important factor in the working dog, and is especially influential in protection training. The pack identity creates the willingness to cooperate with the handler. Pack cooperation creates and strengthens a spirit capable of both fighting together and showing affection toward each other.

A truly social animal.

Dogs show affection to their handler in many ways, most of which we also note in wolf behaviour. The dog will show allegiance to the pack leader by stretching, licking the mouth or face area, nibbling, groin presentation, whining, submissive grins, pushing the muzzle against him, avoidance of eye contact, and wagging the tail, if not the entire body.

As we shall explore further in Chapter 2, problems may occur in the dog/human pack. Within the pack, discipline always exists; either the handler disciplines, or the dog does. If the handler is too lenient or permissive, the dog will feel that he is the 'alpha', or 'top dog'. Such a dog will, in essence, bite the handler to 'correct' his behaviour. In the case of the handler being unable to provide discipline, the dog remains infantile, basking in the handler's indulgence. However, the moment the handler demands that the dog obey, where only indulgence existed before, the dog will strive to remain dominant.

Most dog breeders misunderstand the pack relationship, or ignore it for financial gain. This results in the protective instincts of many breeds being phased out in order to obtain a dog whom even the most uninformed and submissive handler may control. This is the root cause of the demise of the working dog. At the start of the twentieth century the German Shepherd Dog was legendary for its courage and fighting ability, yet it was funny-looking to the general public, and difficult to handle. As the German Shepherd gained media popularity, breeders produced dogs reflecting the market for beauty and submissiveness. The result lacked working temperament, but produced beautiful pets and show animals that anyone may handle. Thus, many genetic lines of today's German Shepherds and Dobermans lack the key attributes of their ancestors.

Command Style

A very prevalent beginner's mistake is to use hand signals in conjunction with voice commands. Voice commands work in darkness, in fog, at a distance, or even if the dog is not looking at you. During sleeve work, the dog uses his eyes to guard and intimidate the helper. For the working dog, the handler must use voice commands exclusively, and refrain from using hand signals. The only exception to this rule is the directional point for the search and the send away, or to provide temporary assistance when teaching a new behaviour.

The competent handler understands his dog fully and uses this understanding to strengthen the team. Such a handler knows when it is time to work the dog, and when it is time to let the dog be a dog. During the dog's time he may pull the handler around by the leash while investigating every smell that appears interesting, and urinating on just about anything and everything that won't disturb people. The term 'team' is bi-directional; communication flows both ways. The dog influences the handler and the handler influences the dog. Yet ultimately, the handler is always in charge, and the dog must know that this is the case.

SUMMARY

In this chapter, we have seen that the working dog is not a trained circus animal, but an animal trained in many situations, and therefore able to apply learned behaviour to new circumstances. The Schutzhund dog is proficient in three interacting areas of behaviour: tracking, obedience and protection. The good working prospect enjoys learning if the trainer applies positive reinforcement. Using positive reinforcement is especially important when teaching new behaviours. A corollary to this is: when teaching the adult dog a new behaviour, use easy training collar corrections. Also, always mix mastered routines with the introduction of new behaviours. This method provides the dog with relief from the confusion created by the new pressure. Remember that the dog performing a behaviour correctly may still not understand what he is doing. As a general rule, the dog who understands displays a joyful demeanour, while the dog who performs without understanding appears confused, timid and submissive. Such a dog does not know *why* he feels corrections, but only their source.

Finally, the key to effective training is observing the dog's behaviour. The handler must identify the body language that shows confusion, excitement, illness, understanding, submission, and dominance. Importantly, we must continue to observe our dog as he ages, for the dog is not static, but dynamic.

CHAPTER TWO

Working Puppies

When beginning the search for that perfect pup, before inspecting a litter be certain to look for a genetic background that reflects a working theme. Any pedigree should reflect Schutzhund (SchH, IPO) or various police (DPH, PH, PSP) or herding (HGH) titles on both the mother's and father's line. (See list of recognized working titles at rear of book.) The livestock herding title (HGH) requires the dog not only to work herding animals, which is extremely difficult work, but also to bite in defence of the handler.

Do not waste time studying scores leading to the titles (if available), for what we want is the genetic evidence that the pup may have the ability to cope with the stresses of learning to work. Therefore, nearly all of the litter's ancestors should have working titles after their names. It is not good enough to be told that one parent was 'a police dog', for many police dogs in the United States are of poor quality, and show little or no evidence of a working background. Again, the entire pedigree should show that the litter's ancestry passed working tests.

Once you arrive to inspect the litter, look for the pup who is bold, alert, and willing to please. Even at the very young age of five weeks it is possible to note the basic personality that will remain throughout life. Therefore, pups who lack spirit, appear fearful, seem very stubborn, are unaware of what is going on around them, or are sensitive to noise or mild corrections may not grow into confident adults.

Remove the first prospect from the litter and place him in a room or yard area that is totally new for the pup. As the pup explores his new environment, fire a round from a starting pistol or a child's cap gun. If the pup is curious about a loud blast of noise, he has both courage and intelligence. (If the breeder often exposes the pup to loud noises, he will not show any reaction whatsoever.) The pup who reacts initially with fear, but recovers and runs to the source of the noise with intense curiosity also scores well on this test. However, the pup who shows fear (runs away), or freezes mid-stride immediately after the loud noise may have poor working character.

An eight-week-old pup, alert and curious.

Some trainers feel that one of the best overall tests for character is simply observing the puppy's natural attitude toward people. For these trainers, an attentive and friendly pup who watches the approach of a stranger is a positive indicator. However, for our purposes, if a pup passes the noise test, and in play bites everything from litter-mates, trousers, rags and toys, to shoes and shoelaces, then that is the one to take, regardless of sex. There is no need even to look at any other pups in the litter, for this pup is the product of a long line of working dogs. The puppy who is unafraid and curious about things (for us, playful biting is a curiosity trait) that strike a cord of fear in other pups, may have the basic character to see it through the rigours of stressful training at the highest levels. This does not mean that the pup should be fearless, but simply able to come back with a sense of curiosity if unhurt – or even with a sense of belligerence, if miffed. Unless subjected to poor training and abusive environments, the trait of curiosity will stay with the pup throughout life. This is the reason why puppy selection is so important.

Puppy Socialization

If the puppy under consideration is over twelve weeks old, you need to enquire how the owner socialized him. Socialization of puppies is very important for setting up parameters of attitude which are conducive to training. Effective socialization produces the important traits of dependency, trainability and intelligence. Fox points out that

> If socialization is delayed (that is, if puppies are not taken as pets before they are about twelve weeks of age) they are difficult to train. Emotional dependency enhances trainability in the dog. We now have evidence from our laboratory studies that adult domestic dogs exhibit more infantile behaviour and dependency toward people than do wild canids raised under the same conditions.[1]

The dependency and trainability (or willingness) traits are the foundation of the dog/handler team. Since effective socialization

[1] Fox 1974, page 65.

promotes helpful working traits, then the socialization history of a twelve-week-old is important. Ineffective or inadequate socialization before the age of twelve weeks inhibits the dog's dependency upon the handler; furthermore, intelligence and willingness become stunted. Let's look closer at various methods of socializing the pup.

The first important factor of socialization is to accustom the pup to strangers. It may not be enough for the pup to see his own human family frequently – he must see many types of people, especially as they walk nearby self-absorbed. While it is sometimes embarrassing, we often stand outside a busy mall or store entrance, with the pup on a leash, and watch people. Start this when the pup is about six or seven weeks of age. Allow people to approach the pup, but don't let them touch him until he has most of his vaccinations. We normally don't allow petting until the pup is about twelve to fourteen weeks old.

On your first trip to start socialization with people, begin some distance away from the busy humans and moving automobiles. Although the pup has probably never shown shyness in the past, he may do so if rushed into an overwhelming situation with myriads of smells, noises, and unusual sights. Therefore, start slow to be safe. As is often the case, it may be necessary to cancel a socialization trip for a very young pup if he is sleeping upon arrival at the site. If so, try again in a few days. If the pup is in his cycle of energy, he may have no difficulty with anything.

The pup learns considerably from people as they walk past or stop and talk about their own dog's experiences. He attends to new voices, unusual smells and strange sights. However, when the pup tires (which, at six or seven weeks old, may be after ten minutes), he may try to avoid approaching joggers or even big, friendly people. If this is the case, return him gently to his crate when possible. Be sure to provide praise on the way back to the automobile and offer water and a small treat. Continue people socialization at least once or twice a week until six months of age. Thereafter, sustain the process as necessary while the pup matures.

The final important factor of socialization is environmental enrichment. Many dogs have plenty of socialization with people, but may lack, or receive too much, external stimulation. The period between five and ten weeks old is a crucial time for environmental enrichment. Within this period, there is also another key period – from the seventh to the tenth week – for adjusting to new stimuli. Pups confined in a cage or kennel during this period will often show fear later in life when taken into new situations. As adults, they often run to their crates when stressed.

Again, up to twelve weeks of age, any lack of socialization and environmental enrichment will produce fear that harms learning and limits potential. On the other hand, any over-stimulation at this age, caused by severe stress from accidents or abusive behaviour, limits potential for identical reasons – that is, fear occurs that limits learning. Even sanctioned stresses such as ear cropping or long distance travel may cause irreparable harm if carried out between seven and ten weeks of age. Thus, during this crucial period, both under- and over-stimulation may create a fearful pup.

Yet pups must be in mildly stressful situations if they are to become top working dogs! Several studies show that *mild* stressors applied to pups produce bold adults. These studies subject the pup to many stressors: mild cold, placing the pup on a board and gently tilting it, and exposure to flashing lights and loud noises. These stresses were applied between birth and five weeks of age. Compared to a control group, the stressed pups showed less worry and fear, and this helped them in problem-solving. Importantly, they were dominant over the non-stressed pups in competitive situations.

Other studies applied mild stress to older pups for a longer period. One experiment simply allowed pups at the age of five, eight, twelve and sixteen weeks to explore an area with several attractions. Each pup had half an hour in which to explore. Researchers found that, as these pups grew older, they explored more than the control group did at sixteen weeks. The control group pups, as compared to the experimental group, simply withdrew or became fearful upon maturity.

The fundamental principle of socialization is that the working dog prospect must have a gradual increase in environmental stress. If no mild age-appropriate stress occurs, then the dog will grow to prefer the environment that lacks stimulation. The dog without confidence will seek his kennel (or his handler's automobile) for security.

Yet, even with a good genetic background, socialization, and puppy tests, a few good prospects remain on the shy side. In some cases play helps them to gain self-confidence. A tug of war with a jute toy or towel will make many pups more responsive and outgoing. Regular grooming may help prevent shyness because such contact establishes a bond of affection and trust.

Importantly, studies show that the environment can affect brain structure itself. One study carried out on rodents reported that:

> If they were simply removed from the nest for three minutes a day for the first five to ten days of life and kept for this time at room temperature, their body temperature fell. This mild stress affects part of the hormonal system of the developing animal...and somehow 'tunes' this system, so that animals exposed to this mild stress early in life are super-animals when they mature – 'super' because they are able to withstand stress better than litter-mates that have not been exposed to this early stress.[2]

This evidence, and other studies, suggest that, with stimulation, the pup's brain grows faster, even larger, than normal. Another study found that doing the opposite, depriving the pup of new situations by raising him in isolation, caused a reduction in rate of brain growth and size.

For very young pups, stimulation means a variety of mild stressors: exposure to mild cold, stroking of the hair, gentle tilting on a surface, and mild visual and auditory surprises. Trainers often confirm that handled pups are far more active and dominant than their non-handled litter-mates. As expected, pups provided with stimuli excelled in problem solving:

> In a learning test in which the pup had to solve simple detour problems, the nonhandled pups were extremely aroused, yelped a good deal and made many errors. They were clearly more emotionally disturbed in the test situation than the handled pups. The latter kept their cool, making few errors and solving the problems very quickly and with little distress vocalization.[3]

[2] Fox,1972, pages 100-1.
[3] Fox, 1972, page 102.

When pups are about two to three weeks of age, the eyes open and serious learning begins. The character of the dog begins to form, and is essentially complete at sixteen weeks of age. As mentioned earlier, the basic characteristics exhibited by young pups tend to remain throughout life. Pups who are aggressive, passive or dependent at four or six weeks are still that way when fully mature. However, there is still room for environmental influences. If the handler is erratic and incompetent, a timid pup will grow more fearful and difficult to handle. The brutal handler may create a disaster for the confident and aggressive pup; this pup may grow into a submissive doormat.

Here, we note the typical problem with a novice handler. That is, the inexperienced and untaught handler tries to correct and control all of the pup's activities. This fearful handler rationalizes over-correction as the only method by which to remain dominant over the growing dog. To the untaught, their control is 'training', but to the pup it can be a form of brutal abuse. For instance, instead of calmly cleaning the mess and making a mental note always to take the pup outside after eating, sleeping or playing to urinate, the handler strikes, yells, or pushes the pup's nose in the mess in order to 'teach him'.

A very common example of handler over-reaction is fearing the pup's use of his mouth. Such a handler cannot bear the sight of teeth, especially if the aggressive pup plays rough. We often hear this handler verbalize his fear by stating that he always corrects the dog when 'his teeth touch skin'. This handler fails to note his contradictory attitude of correcting rough play while simultaneously expressing the desire to own and train a Schutzhund dog. His actions are contrary to what we are trying to do with a working prospect, for we want to build a strong foundation from which to launch training objectives. This foundation is based upon the handler's own training knowledge. As competent trainers know, dogs retain nearly all their learning, both intentional and unintentional. Any new behavioural demand that conflicts with a learned behaviour merely causes profound confusion and training delays.

The working pup will playfully bite just about everything.

Another, less common, scenario is that an aggressive pup brought up by a weak and inexperienced owner may become dominant, growing into an over-aggressive and uncontrollable adult. In this case, the handler is clueless about pack theory. Using a modern psychological theory, this handler believes that the high-powered working pup will respond to 'unconditional love'. Unfortunately, a lot of dogs who find themselves with this type of owner end up in the dog pound.

Even once basic personality is set, dogs may show radical changes in overall behaviour (for better or worse) any time during the first two years of life. Therefore, given a pup with a good genetic working background, we may have a lot of scope to improve or ruin him, depending upon training variables.

Not all stresses appropriate to the pup occur outside the whelping box. During the period between the third and seventh week, pups interact with their mother and litter-mates, forming attachments and establishing a social hierarchy. This is normal, and helps to promote a well-rounded dog. Over-aggression and non-cooperation develop in dogs who are removed from the mother's discipline before five weeks of age. This is especially true of hand-raised pups.

Interaction between individual pups in the litter produces a lasting social hierarchy, with size being important – at least for males (although exceptions certainly do occur). However, if the litter is entirely female, it is not the biggest but the loudest who is often dominant![4]

Puppy play is another factor in determining dominance. Play establishes pecking order relationships, based upon dominance and subordination. This results in violence control within the pack: as each pup realizes his place within the group, aggression reduces. This status quo becomes upset when a group member leaves or a new pup enters, which usually results in fighting and a new dominance hierarchy.

Play also exposes the young dog to varying social situations. Experiencing social roles in the pack, such as being the leader, the follower, the innovator or a cooperative partner is valuable to the puppy in terms of learning social adjustment. Similarly, play provides the pup with an opportunity to explore and manipulate a variety of objects. As we saw earlier, such exploratory behaviour exposes the pup to new situations, thereby providing the necessary experience to tackle future problems. It is exploratory playfulness that hints at a working dog, for there is a high correlation between play and working willingness (trainability).

During the crucial stage that occurs between the fifth and twelfth week, the handler should place the pup in the home. To speed the socializing process, we recommend that handlers fix a leash to a belt loop and go about their daily activities with the pup (while he is full of energy) in tow. (This method is also very effective with newly acquired adult dogs.)

At this time, it is essential to have a couple weeks available in

[4] Pfaffenberger, 1984, page 125.

which to be at home for the pup. This is especially true if you find a good five-week-old pup. You and your spouse must become litter replacements – indeed, from personal experience, we suggest placing the tiny package in bed between oneself and one's spouse for the first few weeks! The pup wears a small leather collar with a lightweight nylon leash. This method provides such security for the pup that we have not had one cry during his first night.

To avoid any potty accidents, take the pup outside in the early morning. If the pup is a German Shepherd Dog, he will begin to run hot between two large humans at about eight weeks. This is the cue for the next step: to place the pup on the floor, tied to the bed. While he is on the floor, continue letting him outside in the early morning hours. The timing for the next step varies, but it is usually around fourteen to sixteen weeks that you will find it impossible to keep the pup off the bed (remember that you want to avoid the use of compulsion as much as possible at a young age). This is where crate training becomes invaluable, for now it is time for the pup to use it for sleeping. The first couple of nights that the pup is in the crate, continue to let him out in the early morning. However, at this stage, you are close to getting your first night of uninterrupted sleep!

The period between twelve and sixteen weeks of age finds the pup pushing for independence; getting into mischief and chewing on just about everything. As the pup bounces, bites and wrestles, he is learning and controlling. This is the time when the handler and dog decide who is boss. If the pup becomes dominant over the handler, then we see the root of a future problem. When a permissively raised pup (a pup who has had no training programme) reaches sexual maturity, he may become more difficult to handle, often showing indifference to the owner, and aggression when disciplined or restrained. However, the handler who keeps the pup on a daily schedule of non-compulsive obedience; supervised play and exercise; tracking and rag work, produces a pup who is dependent upon the handler for leadership and fun. And the dog who sees the handler as a leader will remain dependent, regardless of personality and drives.

A motivated and happy pup.

Starting Training

Now that you selected your pup, where do you start? Well, that depends upon the advice of the particular trainer, and advice does vary. The most important factor in training is determining how to motivate the pup to respond correctly. For the very young pup, (five to twelve weeks) the only way to start is with small pieces of bait $\frac{1}{4}$ inch (6 mm) in diameter. As the pup progresses, slowly replace the bait with a chase toy. Do this by throwing the toy when the pup complies with a training request, and giving bait either when he picks it up or after he returns with it, depending upon his level of training.

Fit the puppy with a leather collar and attach a lightweight leash or line. This should always be on the pup when he is out of the kennel. Indoors or out, the pup should always wear a leash or a small diameter nylon line. You'll find that the leash is an easy way to keep him out of mischief (for example, by tying him temporarily to a fixed object), and an aid in locating where he is. We recommend having two lines, one for outside and the other for inside.

Training periods should take place when the pup is full of energy. What better way to burn off energy than with physical training? For instance, an energetic five-week-old pup may start tracking work by learning to follow a finger touching bait on the floor. This method is a very good way to begin teaching commands. Novice handlers are often astounded when they see pups a few weeks old tracking better than newly initiated adult dogs. Using the kitchen floor for a tracking field, place several pieces of bait in an area 6 in (15 cm) square. From this makeshift bait pad, lay several pieces of bait leading away from the start area. Go ahead and place a right-angle turn in the bait track. Also, don't worry about entering another room with a different floor. We are shaping for future tracking behaviour that will handle changing terrain and turns. You may be surprised to learn that turns and changes in floor coverings (terrain) are not difficult for the pup to master.

With the hungry pup playing with you, point your finger at a piece of bait while softly giving the 'track' command. Over time, the pup simply learns that when he hears this command while simultaneously seeing your finger touch the floor, he will find a piece of food. If you combine the moving finger with a 'track' command, you are shaping behaviour! Touch each piece of bait while giving the command. Once the pup consistently searches for food on command with little help, move outside to the lawn.

For grass conditions, the best time to teach tracking is just before sunrise, while the lawn is still wet from the morning dew. Make a scent pad in the grass about 1 sq. ft (30 cm^2) in size. Don't lay any bait yet. Next, begin your track, but make it easy. We start with laying a trench in the dew-covered grass by sliding our feet in a straight line for about 10–15 ft (3–4.6 m). Go ahead and put a right-angle turn in the track, but vary the direction each day (if today's track turns right, then tomorrow's turns left). At the end of the track, do an about-turn and go over your track again, using the same method. Do another about-turn when you reach the beginning of the track, and get your bait ready. Bait the scent pad with six pieces or more and proceed to bait the entire track every few inches. Since the pup will miss some of the bait, it's best to over-bait to make certain that he will find enough to maintain motivation.

Start the pup on the scent pad, using your finger to point out bait while simultaneously giving the 'track' command. At this point the pup believes this command produces bait wherever your finger is, so if your hand is off the ground, the pup's eyes will leave the track to look for a finger. Go ahead and help him with the finger, but begin to give the 'track' command the moment he is about to find bait on his own. This is crucial, so it bears repeating: the moment the pup independently (without finger help) is about to find bait, give the 'track' command. (Of course, this assumes that the handler sees the bait before the pup does, which should be the case.) Soon, the pup will associate the 'track' command with finding bait instead of following a finger. So far, so good. However, be certain to help him with your finger whenever he gives up or looks to you for help. With daily tracking, the pup will eventually learn that when he stays with the track scent, he will find bait. You now have a beginner tracker. This may occur at less than six weeks old!

Grass tracking for bait at nearly seven weeks old.

This youngster needs no handler help.

The pup has no difficulty going into a right-angled turn.

Learning to sit is almost natural for these dogs. We simply offer a piece of bait (which is held in the hand for other training routines) after the pup sits calmly on his own, and combine this with the 'sit' command. At first, the pup usually jumps and nips at the hand that is holding the bait, but soon gives up jumping and simply sits, looking up and asking for bait, which we provide. After several repetitions of following voluntary sitting with the belated 'sit' command, we then ask him to sit, with the command coming first. It always works. You can use this principle in other areas if the pup happens to do naturally and correctly a behaviour you will need to teach in the future.

The non-compulsive come-on-command is also natural if you have bait. Indeed, since the pup doesn't yet stay, it may be difficult to establish any distance between you and him which would enable you to call him. (There is a way of achieving this which is explained on pages 54–55.) Be certain to provide a reward immediately after you have called him excitingly. Once he understands the 'come' command, then reinforce it intermittently with bait, but *always* reinforce it with the throw toy.

If the pup is beginning to come on command, start ball retrieval shaping close to you, with a leash for the easily distracted, but with self-corrections only. Begin by using a squeaky toy that is roughly in the shape of a ball. With bait at the ready, squeak the toy and toss it a foot or so away while giving the 'bring' command. If the pup goes to it and picks it up, tell him to 'come' while giving exaggerated encouragement. At first, if he merely goes to the toy and picks it up, give him a piece of bait. After several rewards for picking up the toy, withhold the bait until he carries it toward you even a little – then be certain to offer a small piece of bait. Soon the pup will carry the toy all the way.

This principle of training is important, so it bears elaboration. If the pup runs to the toy, picks it up but then drops it, go ahead and reward this behaviour for the first couple of throws, since he is learning in the right direction. The third time he does this do not reward him after he drops the toy, but fetch the toy and toss it a very short distance, then offer bait the moment he picks it up, but before he drops it. After he picks up the toy, back off slowly while giving verbal encouragement for carrying, rewarding each small increase in distance carried just before he drops the toy. Work in this way over several sessions.

Pups can learn the basics of heeling as early as five weeks of age.

With bait in hand, simply give the 'heel' command while showing the bait. You may have to stoop over at first, but this may be unnecessary if the pup already knows from other training experience that you are about to reward him with food. As in all obedience training, at first reward early. For heeling, reward after the puppy has followed only a couple of feet. Gradually build up distance, adding turns and about-turns. Depending upon the intensity of the pup, very light corrective heeling with a training collar may begin between the ages of ten and seventeen weeks. However, good shaping behaviour should make even the slightest training collar correction unnecessary for months.

Although you will not yet use it for corrections, at ten weeks of age place a lightweight training collar on the pup (above the flat leather collar) to accustom him to its feel. We recommend that before ten or so weeks of age, you should use only positive reinforcement in the form of verbal praise and offered bait. After ten to twelve weeks of age, attach the leash to the training collar, but only let the pup gently correct himself. What you don't want is for the pup to become fearful from a sense of being attacked by the training collar, for fear counters trust and all that we're trying to build up. To overcome the problem of fear, at about sixteen weeks, give the pup a very mild training collar correction during the heeling routine, and immediately throw the chase toy, offering plenty of verbal encouragement.[5] If you continue to provide positive reinforcement after a correction, the pup will tolerate corrections and begin to understand what 'correction' means. Use this method of correction until you are certain that the dog knows what you want.

During the heeling exercise, ask the pup to walk over a broom handle. Before he walks or jumps over it, give the 'jump' command, and reward him upon completion. Remember that you are simply shaping the pup for future work, so don't ask him to jump more than two or three inches. The handler must show exaggerated exuberance and always give considerable verbal praise.

Also at five weeks of age we begin to shape behaviour for both the come and the send away. This is a great way to achieve distance

[5] To keep the dog's focus upon yourself, always pull the toy from a pocket or holder. Do not hold the toy whilst training.

between you and the pup for the 'come' command. With the pup looking on, place a piece of bait on your future adult retrieval toy, (ball or Kong®). Place the pup only a few inches away, facing the toy, and release him with the send away command. At first, help him find the bait, as he may be used to looking for it on the floor because of his preliminary tracking experience. When he finds the bait, give the 'come' command excitingly and give him more bait upon arrival. Bait the ball again, but now move away from it a few inches and proceed as before. As the pup masters each new distance, both of you move back, always leaving the ball exactly where it was when you began the routine during the first session. In no time you will have a six-week-old pup running more than 25 ft (8 m) to the target, turning around and running back!

Teach the 'down' once the pup has learned how you teach, that is, once the pup understands that when he does something correct, either he earns bait, or the toy comes out, or both. With the pup in the 'sit' position, kneel in front of him and gently pull out his front limbs while repeating the 'down' command. At first the pup will stand, but be gently persistent. Once you establish the down position, immediately throw the chase toy and reward the pup upon return. If you do this three or four times during the training session, and exhibit exaggerated enthusiasm, the pup will at least go down partially by the third day. By the fifth day he will respond to 'down' from a distance, but he will still not be certain what you want. Therefore, remember to provide praise, toy and bait whenever he responds.

By now the pup is driving the handler crazy with playful, but painful bites and nips. As early as five weeks of age, the handler must provide an outlet for biting with rag play. Gradually the pup will learn to confine biting behaviour to the rag and, eventually, the sleeve. Remember that puppy muscles are developing, therefore be careful not to hurt the pup. Also, before sixteen weeks or so, the teeth are sharp enough to go through just about anything, making it hard for the pup to release. Early on, (five to eight weeks of age) as the pup bites the rag, watch the grip to see if he is trying to release. If so, then reduce the rag pressure on the mouth until he re-bites, then release it so that he will win. With practice, the pup will become more secure on the rag, but always watch the grip. If it is weak, back-off on the rag pressure.

Always let the pup win the rag and carry it off, only to restart the game after he drops it. Never win a rag fight with the pup, as this is contrary to what we are trying to achieve with a future protection dog. Also, do not ask the pup to bring the rag back to you, as retrieval is a separate exercise. What you don't want to do is mix obedience with bite work at this point. However, try giving the 'out' command with plenty of praise when he drops the rag on his own, but use no compulsion whatsoever. Between the ages of fourteen and fifteen weeks increase rag work intensity if teething is not yet a problem. Once teething begins, reduce rag play frequency and intensity. Do not cease rag play, but be careful not to cause pain.

Continue rag work with the pup until around ten months of age, depending upon the individual. When he is biting strongly with the helper, slowly introduce the soft puppy sleeve. Have the decoy rag play for a few bites, then place the rag over the sleeve, if necessary. The decoy merely acts as though the sleeve and rag were no different from the rag alone, and the pup may not notice a visible difference. Use both the rag and puppy sleeve for a few sessions: eventually the pup will have no problem biting the sleeve.

Up to about ten to fourteen months of age, the pup should be only prey biting. (See Chapter 4 for definitions of prey and defence biting.) After this age, if the pup is consistently biting the sleeve with power, defence biting may safely begin. This is a crucial moment, so do not rush the pup into defence work. The pup must not feel enough pressure to induce fear, as Barwig relates:

> When the puppy has reached ten to twelve months of age, I start to transfer the biting to the defence drive by doing civil agitation and presenting slight threats to the dog. As the dog is being switched to the defence mode, we are careful not to overstress him. Confidence building is being done continually. Once he feels threatened and shows aggression, the helper should immediately retreat. Care must be taken so that the dog is not overloaded with pressure.[6]

Once the pup grows accustomed to defence biting, and is biting full and hard, learning to release (the 'out') is the next step. Details

[6] Barwig, 1986, page 549.

of this procedure are given in Chapter 4. It is at this point that compulsive obedience work (dumb-bell work) begins as well.

It is no coincidence that compulsive obedience work begins at around the time the dog shows increasing aggression. This aggression often occurs between the ages of twelve and twenty-four months. Such behaviour comes from increasing maturity and bite work. As the dog begins to challenge his handler, or simply becomes more stubborn, the handler uses obedience demands to maintain the alpha position. Be prepared to use some strong leash work in some cases.

The Portable Kennel

Transporting your working dog in a lightweight crate is an irony of dog training. If the dog is sitting in the back seat when your local car-jacker strikes, he may be of some help. This is not the case when placed in the crate. On the other hand, one of these high-powered dogs may virtually crash through a car window when something exciting appears. Further, a dog in a travelling kennel has some protection if there is a road accident. Therefore, working dog trainers recommend teaching the pup to crate upon command.

Unless you have a puppy-proof house, the crate will also keep him out of trouble when there is no time to supervise. The crate may go in the bedroom at night, the garage in the morning, or under a tree during nap time. You can take it wherever you go, which is important during the socialization period. Furthermore, the crate is useful for house-training: usually dogs will not relieve themselves inside the crate.

The rule regarding crate size is to get one big enough for the adult dog to comfortably turn around in. Crates now come in sizes that range from toy to giant breeds.

Training the pup to enter the portable kennel eagerly takes very little time. Leaving the door open, throw a toy or a treat inside, and combine this with the command to enter (most trainers say 'kennel up'). If the pup goes in, do not close the door, but let him come out on his own, rewarding and praising him for his courage. Repeat this technique for a few days, depending upon the dog. The next step is

Crates.

to ask the pup to enter without the treat or toy, but giving him a reward after he enters. Some trainers give the pup attention only when he enters the kennel, otherwise ignoring him.

Once the pup enters without hesitation, it is time to introduce the door. With him inside, close the door, praise and reward him, then open the door and provide a play session. Gradually increase the time for which the door remains closed in two- to five-minute increments. When a thirty-minute period elapses with no problems, begin to leave the house for short periods and have a play session upon returning.

Some trainers calculate the puppy's age in months as equal to the number of hours for crate containment. Thus, the five-month-old pup gets out after five hours. Except during kennel training, before the pup enters the crate, be certain that it is only after exercise and elimination. Immediately upon his release, lead him outside to his favourite urination area. Pups normally eliminate after sleeping, eating, drinking, playing, walking, or even being petted. Therefore, take him outside on a leash after these activities and gently give the elimination command.

Aerobic Exercise

If the pup is physically willing, begin walking him at around eight weeks old. In the beginning, start on the short side and evaluate how the pup is responding. Begin with walks of about half a mile (0.8 km) and work up to nearly 2 miles (3.2 km), the latter distance usually occurring at around twelve weeks of age. Depending upon the pup, we discontinue walking and begin using the bicycle at around sixteen weeks of age.

There are a couple of commercial products on the market that help control the dog while the handler is on the bike. We recommend using a product called a 'Springer'. This unit prevents the dog from getting in front of or under the wheels, while allowing him some flexibility of movement. Be certain to attach the Springer to the flat collar, as the dog will pull. There are two items of importance to mention. First, remember to not allow the dog to move faster than a trot. A trot is usually less than 14 mph (22 kph) for large, long-legged breeds such as the Doberman. Second, if trotting

The bicycle 'Springer'.

on asphalt or concrete, you must check the dog's pads less than 2 miles (3.2 km) out. This is especially important if the dog is in excellent condition for dirt roads, since he will look good even when the pads begin to bleed from wear. Exposure of pads to hard surfaces must build up slowly just as conditioning must increase gradually. When checking pads, simply stand over the dog and gently bend each foot at the wrist. Look for any signs of small, dark points. The pad should look almost chalky white, but with non-conditioned wear, blood will darken the whiteness.

By the time the pup is twenty weeks old, he is trotting about 2½ miles (4 km) nearly four times a week. If the dog is in good health, we recommend trotting this distance at least three times a week.

A good working prospect.

SUMMARY

Before looking at a litter, find out if the genetic background is predisposed to work. Remember that the pup's personality is set by the age of sixteen weeks. Prior to this age, studies show that various mild stressors increase brain size, confidence and willingness (trainability). However, abuse or over-stimulation creates the same result as under-stimulation, that is to say, fear. Begin informal non-compulsive training during periods of high energy, as early as five weeks. Early training is important, for several studies show that within the sixteen week period of socialization, there appears to be an 'imprinting' stage in dogs similar to that in birds.

There are two factors of socialization: people and environment. In general, the more exposure there is to these two factors, the more likely the pup is to grow into a confident adult. However, environmental over-exposure may be as detrimental as under-exposure, both creating a fearful adult. Therefore, it is essential to watch the pup closely while introducing a new stimulus slowly. For instance, if the twelve-week-old pup responds to a slight training collar correction with fear and tries to run away, then cease any form of correction and wait for maturity to assist training.

CHAPTER THREE

Obedience Training

We often hear non-competitive handlers question the value of teaching tracking and various obedience routines if they have no interest in trials. Although we touched upon this point earlier, it's worth some elaboration. Having a protection dog is work for both the dog and the handler. The good protection dog develops from the working interaction that occurs between the various behaviours leading to the mastering of tracking, obedience, and protection. However, mutual working goes beyond mere correction and reinforcement in these areas. Handlers must visualize themselves as psychologically reaching out to the dog, in a way similar to a parent who gently, but persistently, knocks on an autistic child's mind. When the door opens, understanding occurs and behaviour becomes predictable for both the handler and the dog. Remember, there are two minds, and two doors, creating a learning situation for both members of the team. The handler learns to read the dog by observing behaviour displayed in the three areas of learning, while the dog learns to confidently evaluate an environment that includes the handler. Shared learning creates a rare spirit, which is beautiful to behold.

Such fashionable words as 'bonding' fail to label correctly the unspoken interaction between the team. Indeed, this word confuses understanding, because we unconsciously use the word to view the dog growing closer to us, rather than each growing toward the other. This results in viewing the dog as an ego extension, therefore setting up the imperfect dog and human for failure, since all modern egos idolize perfection.

How, then, is 'team' defined? There is an uncomplicated reason for the handler to participate in training the dog, rather than hiring someone else to do the training, or purchasing a trained dog. It is the fact that teaching the dog compels the handler to learn. The only way to achieve this learning, that we know of, is for dog and handler to learn from each other. It is the work that goes into all phases of training, combined with kindness, understanding and patience (essentially, maturity) that produces the team's shared spirit of accomplishment. These areas of training, for the most part, are not new, but come to us from the peasant Germans who lived in the latter years of the nineteenth century.

Before the formation of organized protection dog clubs, this self-reliant people cultivated the handler/dog spirit, not for winning dog trials, but for aiding the struggle for survival. German farm dogs were playmates for children, herded and tracked lost sheep and cattle, defended chickens and goats from strays and predators, and protected families from recalcitrant drunks and robbers. While their methods of training were crude by today's standards, these people did indeed show the true value of the working dog, bequeathing us the three building blocks that lead to strong character and a well-rounded dog, regardless of breed.

As noted earlier, responsible ownership of a working dog is demanding. Preparing the competition dog is even more exacting. Unfortunately, complete control over a dog in every behavioural nuance is the nature of competition today. Highly competitive handlers demand that the dog responds perfectly (that is, sitting perfectly; constantly looking at the handler's face during heeling; not playing with the dumb-bell; perfect finish; jumping cleanly, etc.).[1] However, mere *general* control is all that is necessary for the genuine working dog. Such general control has the handler expecting, and getting, obedience from the dog with the added benefit of the dog displaying individual thinking. For instance, the competition dog learns never to expect an attack sequence during the obedience phase. This allows the dog to remain alert to the handler only. On the other hand, the trained protection dog not only expects an attack, but looks for the place where it may happen.

[1]MacInnes offers: 'The writer deplores the trend of obedience tests in this country to turn the dog into an automaton, the precision of his performance being everything to some judges, and very little attention being paid to the underlying character and intelligence of the dog'. 1955, page 70.

Therefore the protection dog not only remains alert to his handler, but to the environment as well (even though he is scored lower by the Schutzhund judge who, nevertheless, insist that protection is a serious business). Reality-based general control produces a working dog capable of independent thinking, with the ability to pass the pre-competitive training test of Schutzhund. Therefore, the form of obedience training this handbook teaches does not promote a robotic, dumbed-down or submissive dog, but one who incorporates a playful attitude, mixed with confident seriousness if the situation arises.

Obedience for the Working Dog

During the first few weeks of life, the pup undergoes various behavioural shaping strategies designed for biting, tracking and obedience. When does formal obedience begin? Obedience begins whenever the pup becomes a full-time monster! Recall that the goal of puppy selection was to meet several criteria: high energy, curiosity, and courage. While these traits are desirable in the well-trained adult dog, in the pup, they make living conditions terrible. What better way to use this high-spirited energy than to begin mild, non-compulsive obedience, rag work and tracking?

The use of training collar corrections depends upon the dog's age. When introducing a new behavioural demand for the adult dog, we can mix together positive reinforcement and mild training collar corrections. However, if we are considering the young pup of six weeks up to six months of age, there are very few moments when a training collar correction is necessary. All that is necessary for the young pup with high drive is patience, plenty of bait and a couple toys: 'instant training' must not be the handler's expectation.

For example, using only positive reinforcement, we began working with a pup at just over five weeks old. At twenty-three weeks of age the pup, still with almost no training collar corrections, could heel very well with left and right turns, left about-turns, fast and slow speed changes; could perform sit-in-motion; come on command from thirty paces; go down on command; search two blinds; track four hundred paces with turns in a disced field, and do the send away at forty paces (without downing). Oddly, this pup really did not have a clue as to what she was doing, but she loved chase toys and bait. The right training tools and techniques promote early learning.

Every new task is broken down to its smallest behavioural element with immediate reinforcement with the throw toy and/or food, depending upon the age of the pup. Later, the training collar may be necessary as the pup matures and becomes more independent – this is especially the case with males.

To put in another way, when beginning a new behavioural goal, always break down the routine into several sub-elements, making them exclusive from the total behaviour. Each broken down element fits into the final product. This is another form of shaping. Most importantly, do not try to hurry the dog to learn. Depending upon the task, it may take the dog two to four sessions before he shows a hint of understanding.

It is most important to reinforce this first hint of desired behaviour, no matter how sloppy or incomplete. However, the hint of compliance is not the key to training: this is the immediate reinforcement of showing the desired behaviour when the pup or dog is in a totally confused state of mind. What we mean here is that, when teaching the youngster to 'down', (working from a sit) the handler gently pulls the front legs out while giving a mild command to down. The handler must reinforce the pup's acceptance of physical handling as a first step. Therefore, the pup, at first, gets the toy or bait for allowing the handler to gently pull the front legs out – even if the hindquarters rise. On the third session, he gets the bait for allowing the handler to physically put him in a 'down'. It is at this point that the dog begins to understand what the sympathetic handler is trying to teach, and he may show this by going down without the handler's physical help in the next session (but with the handler's animated voice and hand signals).

Use over-reinforcement in all sub-routines when teaching new behaviours. That is, provide bait or the chase toy for any hint of learning. Continue combining this method of reinforcement with breaking down routines into sub-routines. For instance, teach separately the come on command; the front sit; and the finish to the side (the latter for older pups).

It is important to understand that shaping begins at any point, not simply at the beginning of a routine. Therefore, you may start by teaching the sub-behaviour that ends the routine, rather than the beginning. For example, teaching the front sit before the come. This may be especially helpful when teaching a new behaviour that is similar to one already mastered, which may be the result of unintentional shaping. Therefore, we teach the front sit since the dog may know how to sit for food. The only limitation of shaping creativity is the trainer's imagination.

Shaping the five-week-old puppy for tracking occurs when using the 'track' command and pointing at the bait. In very little time, the pup learns to lower his nose to ground level in response to seeing the finger touch the floor and hearing the command. With proper shaping techniques, the dog begins to understand that he has only one option: to comply. In the example above, the pup learns that compliance to the tracking command produces bait.

Once a dog has learned a new behaviour, and has practised it often, there is never an instance during training when he does not understand that this behaviour is expected. The reason for this is that dogs will not forget consistent good training. This is the major difference between effective and incompetent training: consistency. The working dog handler expects – and depending upon the age of the dog – even demands, obedience. By contrast, the typical pet owner is happy when the dog responds occasionally.

On the other hand, consistency does not mean that the dog must, without fail, comply with a command before receiving something he wants. Mysteriously, novice handlers are forever recalling from somewhere that they must make a slave of the dog by making him work for everything. This is not the case at all, and perhaps is another form of abusive treatment. It is important for the dog to have time with the handler when he can remain simply a dog. Thus, the handler need not feel guilt about wanting to give the four-legged friend a piece of leftover sandwich without placing the dog in some obedience routine, no matter how small.

Now is a good time to review training terms. Verbal and physical praise, food and toys, are reinforcers for behaviour. When used after the desired behaviour occurs, they are called 'positive reinforcers'. Therefore, throwing the chase toy after the dog does something correctly, however minor it may be, increases the chances of the behaviour occurring again.

A 'correction' ceases a behaviour. Punishment, or a correction, is a verbal reprimand or the use of the correction collar. Corrections work only when used *immediately* after the undesirable behaviour.

'Negative reinforcement' is distinct from punishment in that it also increases the desired behaviour. Once the dog understands that the training collar will constrict when he forges ahead, he stays at your side. In this case, mild self-punishment begins the technique, but negative reinforcement keeps him at your side to avoid future training collar effects. Another example of negative reinforcement to which we may all relate is the behaviour of opening an umbrella before stepping into heavy rain. Opening the umbrella becomes negatively reinforced with the threat of getting wet.

Voice tone is another form of negative reinforcement. When a serious command tone occurs simultaneously with a correction, the future stage is set for negative reinforcement. Avoidance of the correction reinforces the desired behaviour. The dog learns that failure to comply with a particular voice tone may result in a correction.

The dog knows from past training, puppy or otherwise, that corrections do not occur when the handler uses an excited or high-pitched voice tone. There may be many other situations around the home where the dog learned from voice tone that strict compliance was not necessary. However, just as he has learned when compliance is not necessary, he also must learn when he *must* comply, as a working dog should. Therefore, after the adult dog has learned a desired behaviour, use a command voice coupled with a mild correction. Soon, tone alone may be all that is necessary to guide the dog. This voice is without yelling, screaming, pleading or pity. Rather it shows strength and dominance, both of which are important in the pack relationship. Trainers who understand voice tone reduce their use of obedience training collar corrections, thus maintaining trust and reducing confusion.

It is important to mention scheduling of the reward. 'Scheduling' is how often to throw the chase toy or offer the jute sausage. When the dog is first learning a technique, offer the reward immediately after he does part of it correctly. However, once progress occurs, provide the reward intermittently. For instance, when he is learning to heel off leash, give the reward after he stays at your side for perhaps 10 ft (3 m). As the dog catches on, hold back the reward until he does a turn. Occasionally, return to the early reward schedule, reinforcing every correctly completed small behaviour. With this method, the entire training process becomes great fun – although it may take ten minutes to get through a heeling routine with all the toy-time.

If a chase toy is used for reinforcement, we must mention handler behaviour upon the return of the rewarded dog. Do not make the return another training exercise; take all training pressure off the dog by allowing him to run around the yard for a few moments before calling him back, if necessary. When he comes to you, allow him simply to be at your side while he chews or plays with the toy for a few seconds. Then ask him to 'out' the toy on the ground or in your hand. The idea is that you want him to relax and play as a reward for doing a good job. You do not want him to drop the toy immediately when he reaches your side, because he will slowly increase delay time before returning to you. Ideally, the dog will go out and return fast with the toy.

Whether positive or negative, verbal reinforcement is the trainer's most important tool. When the pup is doing something correctly, tell him and keep telling him as long as he is doing the routine right, just as you do when verbally coaching during tracking. Verbal reinforcement connects the three areas of training and provides for the dog enhanced meaning to the task at hand, even in the likelihood that he is without a clue as to what he is actually doing. During obedience practice, some trainers combine verbal reinforcement with clapping their hands. This may look funny to observers, but you're not there for them.

Again, in all phases of obedience, break each routine, or goal, into several sub-routines and goals. Beside making learning easier for the dog, it keeps him from anticipating commands and retains interest, since the trainer can juggle sub-goals into different orders depending upon the session.

The down-in-motion is a good example of making sub-routines from the total obedience behaviour. One mini-routine is simply downing the dog whilst heeling, with the handler remaining at the dog's side. Without heeling, the second sub-routine is to put the dog in a long 'down', walk a distance of thirty paces, turn and call him. A third routine (that will also assist the send away) is teaching him to go down anywhere in the yard. Make separate routines for the front sit and side finish. Finally, begin a session with heeling, slowing to 'down' the dog, then proceed two or three feet before rewarding. You are now able to build from this foundation, while reducing the dog's confusion. There is no reason to force the dog to learn the entire routine at one time.

Mini-routines may be very subtle. For instance, during the sit-in-motion (described later in this chapter), the handler may throw the reinforcing toy either immediately after the sit, or at any time up to returning to the dog's side. Therefore the dog never knows when the toy will come, thus fixing his attention upon the handler. Using the same routine, sometimes hold the toy in your hand, giving the 'sit' command with a mild correction, throwing the toy immediately upon the sit. The correction increases the speed of the sit, and the toy reinforces the speedy sit. In no time the dog will sit quickly, fitting nicely into the total routine. Rare is the time that the chase toy comes out once at the end of the routine. Therefore, use plenty of toy reinforcement.

The following is a guideline for beginning obedience training that fits into a Schutzhund protection dog's total training. Remember that the handler is the trainer, so feel free to analyse the desired behaviour in order to come up with your unique way of shaping. All shaping must take into account past learned behaviours and those desired for the future. Make all training fun, with lots of toy reinforcement and occasional corrections. At first, progress will seem slow because the dog does a lot of toy chasing, but this is what you want. You want to create an environment in which the dog may learn, and a play environment does indeed teach all willing dogs.

Heeling

The heeling routine consists of left about-turns, right turns, fast, slow and normal speed changes, one stop with a sit and walking a figure of eight in a small group of people. In the first two Schutzhund tests, the routine occurs twice, both on and off leash, with two gunfire shots during the latter.

Heeling is a difficult exercise that forces the dog to maintain attention. Therefore, teaching the routine involves more than going through a few sub-routines, but also teaching the dog to maintain alertness and not to walk with an ears-down submissive look that comes from over-correction. With the training collar in place, start the dog heeling in a straight line with a playful, encouraging command combined with a mild pop of the leash, if necessary. If the dog heels and pays attention for only three steps, throw the chase toy. Begin heeling again and if he stays at your side whilst paying attention, throw the toy after five or so steps. Continue this method through all heeling phases of sitting, left about-turns, right and left turns, speed increase and decrease, and the figure of eight. The point here is to make the dog learn through having great fun chasing his toy.

When you do your first right turn, give a mild pop of the training collar, if necessary, and throw the toy after the turn. Don't forget verbal reinforcement. Given an adult dog who may need a correction, remember to provide often some form of positive reinforcement (verbal, toy or light physical stroke) after the correction when teaching a new behaviour.

With the adult dog, once he has the basics of heeling, start working on maintaining his attention, if necessary. Put the dog on a loose lead and allow him to lead whilst wandering slowly about the field. Allow the dog to smell objects and become distracted. After a short time, when he looks away, make a right turn, giving a mild correction along with the 'heel' command. After a few sessions of this, the dog will keep close attention on the handler. Next, combine this with the basic heeling exercise. On a loose leash, begin heeling with eye contact. Mix this with giving the chase toy when he maintains eye contact and heeling for a short time. Also,

Above left: *Distracted heeling.*

Above right:*A right-angle turn produces a very mild correction.*

Left: *Immediate improvement.*

remember to use verbal praise. When the dog looks away, take a quick step to the right and give a mild correction. As the dog gives eye contact, immediately provide physical praise. Over a period of many sessions, increase the time for which eye contact is demanded.

When the dog is heeling satisfactorily on the lead, hook another lead to the collar. With two leads working the dog, this will complicate your training. Use the two leads for a few heeling sessions. Finally, with two leads on the collar, dramatically take one lead off and make a small show of placing it on the ground. Start heeling with the attached lead being ready to use mild corrections, the chase toy, and plenty of physical and verbal praise. When you remove the first lead, you surprise the dog with the second lead attached to the training collar. This method sets up off-lead heeling.

After using the two-lead method for a few sessions successfully, try off-lead heeling immediately after doing a short on-lead routine. Do not be surprised if the dog heels off-lead exactly as when on-lead. Be sure to play with the chase toy often during the routine. Don't be afraid to replace the lead immediately to account for any individual problems. If problems develop with wide turns or attention deficit, simply hook the lead onto the collar and perform the sub-routine with mild corrections, using toy rewards for doing the job correctly.

We do not always ask the dog to heel whenever he goes out on-lead. Our dogs pull, trot around us in a circle, and lift a leg on just about everything. Therefore, the dog learns that the lead does not necessarily signal work and corrections, but only that he is to remain nearby while still being a dog. It helps to remember that these dogs are not mechanical robots.

The Sit- and Down-in-motion

Introduce both of these exercises in the same way. Start on-lead heeling and stop while giving the 'sit' or 'down' command. For the adult dog, give a quick, but mild, correction. Throw the chase toy. Next, repeat the same routine, but this time walk two feet (60 cm) further after he sits. Be sure to give the mild over-correction with the training collar, combined with the 'sit' command before you walk out a couple of feet. If the dog stays, throw the toy. When he begins to comply without correction as you move away from him, immediately provide the chase toy. This way he begins to learn that the faster he complies, the faster the toy comes out. With familiarity, do the exercise off-lead, mixing the distance between short and long, up to thirty paces, sometimes turning about to the face the dog, and occasionally returning to his side. Again, use the chase toy often for reinforcement as you work up to the total routine.

Teaching the sit-in-motion

With heavy use of the toy, there is no problem with teaching both the sit- and down-in-motion during the same training session, but at first don't do them consecutively. That is, don't do a sit-in-motion, followed by a down-in-motion. Do one sit routine, then go on to a short heel routine, followed by a down-in-motion routine. The handler must read the dog accurately, in order to understand if confusion exists and come up with an alternative plan if problems arrive. Usually, the confused dog will go down when he should sit, or try to follow the handler. In this case, give a few verbal 'no's' and calmly go back and put the dog in sit (or down) exactly where he was originally asked to do so. Next, repeat the routine but shorten the steps taken after the 'sit' command to two or three. Remember to throw the chase toy when the dog does it correctly.

For the sit-in-motion, work up to a minute of sitting while staying at the thirty pace distance. The complete routine calls for the handler to return to the dog's side. In all returns the handler may go to the dog's right or left to walk behind him in order to reach the 'heel' position.

Recall

Like the sit-in-motion, this routine begins with the dog heeling for ten steps, followed by the down-in-motion. The handler continues in a straight line for thirty paces, stops and turns about. The handler gives the 'come' command and the dog should come in fast to a frontal sit. After three seconds, the 'finish' command to the side completes the routine.

During any phase of recall work, do *not* immediately correct the dog when he breaks a stay to approach you; this only confuses the novice dog about the 'come' command. With the adult dog, the correction occurs while the handler replaces the dog in the exact location where the infringement occurred. The method of correction depends upon the dog's level of understanding. If he understands, then perhaps a rather humiliating return by the collar is necessary. However, if the entire procedure is new, merely return the dog without physical or verbal reinforcement and try again, but stay close and keep the long line on his training collar. Upon his breaking the stay, reel him in with the line, telling him 'No, no, no', etc., on your way back to the exact location.

Most inappropriate corrections may cause a slow intentional recall, or worse, fear to approach. With this in mind, there may be certain exceptions for some dogs. The handler must make a judgement based upon the dog's total level of learning and performance. As an example, one of our dogs knows how to do the send away and down.

Yet one day he failed to go down and came straight back to sit perfectly in front, exactly like the recall. Since this occurred, of all times, during a trial, it was not possible to correct him on the spot. Two days later, during send away practise, the dog refused to go down and headed back, despite repeated commands. This time, he was met with a throw chain, which hummed past his head, effectively putting him into the down position.[2] This approach might cause a problem with some dogs in teaching them to 'come'. However, this dog understood the send away, the down, and the recall. Since then, during practise and at another trial, he has completed the send away with no problem and, very importantly, no slowing on the recall.

If you desire to have the dog come directly to you for the front sit (as is necessary for Schutzhund trials), seldom perform the side finish in conjunction with the recall. A slow come, or a poor front sit, or an automatic side-sit will result when the handler always uses a compulsive finish. When the dog does something frequently, he will anticipate and attempt to skip steps. For instance, the dog will run to the handler and do a finish side-sit instead of sitting in front. Therefore, in a separate routine, begin working on the side finish using a 6 ft (2 m) line. Simply place the dog in a sit position and step in front, close enough for his nose to be touching your leg. Give the 'heel' command and lead him to your side, giving the chase toy. Some trainers combine the command with taking one step back with the left foot. Remember not to expect perfection – you are in the shaping stage – so throw the toy when he at first heels only partially to your side from the front sit. As he gets the idea, use mild corrections to increase speed.

Use the 6 ft (2 m) line also to teach the front sit from a 'come' command, if necessary. Place the dog in a down position, take a few steps and turn about to face him. With the chase toy in your hand (or a small piece of bait if the dog is too high in drive to keep away from the toy), call him and give him the 'sit' command as he nears. Reward a sit, no matter how sloppy. After he learns to sit in front without being given the 'sit' command, there will be future sessions for obtaining clean sits.

[2]Most 1955, page 93.

Whether the dog is retrieving or not, start the recall on the long line, working close. Place the dog in a down-stay, take a few steps, stop and face him. Without concerning yourself about the front sit, call him and throw a ball behind you just before he arrives. It is most important to remember that if the dog comes without a command, you do not reward him with the toy. Instead, merely lead him back to the exact spot with verbal 'no's' or mild corrections (depending upon the dog's level of training) during the trip. Perform five or six repetitions, varying the distance with each success.

Up to this point, the dog is not sitting in front, but coming in fast looking for the toy. Go back to the 6 ft (2 m) line and do the recall from the down, bringing him in front whilst giving the 'sit' command. Immediately after the sit, throw the chase toy. Remember not to worry about perfect sits, or combining the separate side finish routine. Gradually increase the distance, still asking him to sit in front. After a few sessions, begin to mix up recalls with the sit in front and omitting the sit by throwing the toy behind you on his approach. This mixing-up will keep his speed up.

Over a period of months, progress should be such that the long line becomes unnecessary and the dog comes in fast and performs the front sit. However, still perform the finish only occasionally, mostly keeping it as part of the sub-routine at any level of training.

Building upon the above work, concentrate upon speed by using distance, the toy and keeping the dog guessing. After placing him in a down or sit-stay, take about fifteen paces and turn to face him. After a couple of seconds, call him and throw the chase toy behind yourself just as the dog nears you. Again, this will keep him coming in fast. Occasionally, keep the toy hidden and ask him to perform a front sit as he nears you. If he starts to slow then stop asking for the sit and throw the toy. Soon he will learn always to come in hard since he believes the toy might come out.

Within the routine, play with your dog by keeping him guessing. We often down the dog and immediately reward his speedy reaction. During the next attempt, we might walk the required thirty paces, wait about twenty seconds and then give the 'come' command. As he nears, we vary between throwing the toy behind or simply standing still, which is his cue to sit in front for an immediate toy reward. In the next session we may again down the dog in motion, this time taking about fifteen paces and, without turning about, offering the chase toy while still walking. The dog always knows that he will be offered the toy, but he never knows when. This maintains alertness and playfulness, so use this template with other routines.

Gunfire

The very young pup should be subjected to various loud noises that are non-threatening, ranging from banging pots together to firing a cap gun or starting pistol while he plays. 'Non-threatening' means to create the noise from a distance, or another room. The handler must not run up to the pup or dog while creating a racket. If pups experience loud noises from three weeks old, they soon show an extreme tolerance and indifference toward all normally disturbing sounds.

When dealing with an adult dog, use verbal, physical and toy encouragement. During practice heeling sessions, have an assistant fire rounds from a distance. As a round is fired every few seconds, play with the dog and praise him. If he tries to run away, allow it, stop the gunfire, and retreat with the dog to a distance where he no longer shows fear. Dragging the dog toward the gunfire may cause further severe training problems.

The goal of gun training, like other areas of training, is reachable by encouragement. Assuming the dog trusts the handler, using play, praise and physical reinforcement leads to the understanding that gun reports will not cause harm. Depending upon the dog, the timescale for acceptance of gunfire may range from immediately to several weeks. However, if abused by incompetent training, he may never overcome gunfire avoidance. (Therefore, gunfire reaction is an important consideration when buying a dog.)

For Schutzhund testing purposes, gunfire occurs twice: once during the off-lead heeling and once during the long 'down' while another dog is heeling. Each occurrence entails two rounds from a 6 mm starting pistol. Gunfire during heeling is normally easy for the dog, since he is concentrating upon the work at hand. However, there is more pressure on the idle dog during the long 'down', for the dog is thinking about his distant handler, the nearby heeling team, and the gunfire. Preparation for the long 'down' with gunfire is similar to gunfire during heeling. After downing the dog, the handler stays nearby while the assistant fires a round from the opposite side of the field. After a few seconds, the handler returns to begin a play session. The time interval between the last report and the play session should be gradually increased. Once the dog becomes accustomed to gunfire, use it during various routines. Given a progressing dog, the more gun reports he hears, the more he learns that there is no reason to fear.

Retrieving the Dumb-bell

The dumb-bell retrieve is probably the most unpopular aspect of Schutzhund and police training. Many former Schutzhund people still training protection dogs comment negatively upon the forced retrieve. However, dumb-bell work lays important foundations in several ways. Between the ages of twelve and twenty-four months, the high-powered working dog begins to test and challenge his handler. This is the opportune time to teach the compulsive retrieve, for dumb-bell work tempers the emerging personality. Second, dumb-bell work leads to retrieval of other objects. Some police departments teach gun retrieval; we know one home owner who taught his dog to find and retrieve any house or car key upon command. Many tracking dogs retrieve articles. The point here is that all difficult retrieval begins with dumb-bell work. The dog learns that he must carry the dumb-bell, which in not an easy task.

The goal of the exercise is to approach, take and return the thrown dumb-bell. The dumb-bell is not like a toy to most dogs, therefore the teaching technique uses compulsion. What makes the exercise difficult to teach is that it is stressful to both the dog and handler. Furthermore, it is the only exercise where the dog may experience genuine surprise and confusion because the method of teaching is unusual for the dog.

That's the bad news. The good news is that, with handler determination, progress is quick, and after the initial shock, fun. First, back-tie the dog on the *flat collar*. The handler has a lead connected to the *correction collar*. The dog is at the end of the back-tie lead with the handler ready to place pressure on the training collar. The back-tie produces the leverage used by the handler to create discomfort for the dog.

Flat collar attached to back-tie and pinch collar attached to lead.

With the lead in one hand and the dumb-bell in the other, offer the dumb-bell to the dog by positioning it near his nose. When he refuses to take it, slowly apply pressure to the correction collar, while offering the dumb-bell with an encouraging 'take it' command. When the dog opens his mouth, quickly place the dumb-bell inside *while letting up on the correction collar pressure*. Just as quickly, praise the dog before he releases the dumb-bell. Usually the dog will spit out the dumb-bell the moment there is no collar pressure. Nevertheless, it is important not to maintain collar pressure when the dog has the dumb-bell. When the dog drops the dumb-bell, build up pressure on the correction collar while again offering the dumb-bell. When the dog takes and holds the dumb-bell for a few seconds, offer praise and play with him with the chase toy. That's enough for one day.

Taking the dumb-bell within the back-tie arc.

Do the same with the next session. Soon, the dog will keep the dumb-bell, forcing you to ask for it back. Usually this is no problem, but some dogs don't want the collar pressure, so they hang on to it. Do not correct the dog with collar pressure when he refuses to release the dumb-bell. Usually a light bump on the nose or chin will cause the release.

During the next few sessions the dog learns to take the dumb-bell from the hand and to release it back into the hand. The next step is getting the dog to take the dumb-bell from the ground. Still on the back-tie, flat collar and correction collar, hold the dumb-bell close to his nose and ask him to take it. Over the next few sessions, slowly increase the distance from his nose, while asking him to take it, until he is picking up the dumb-bell from the ground. When the dog refuses the dumb-bell, use correction collar pressure, being certain that the pressure is off when the dog takes the object.

The next step is retrieving the dumb-bell whilst on the back-tie. Using the back-tie arc for the retrieval space, have the dog at your side, throw the dumb-bell a couple of feet and immediately step toward it, giving the 'take' command. When the dog picks it up, give a lot of encouragement and play. Be ready to provide pressure to the correction collar if the dog drops or refuses the dumb-bell.

The last step involves taking the back-tie off and using only the leash and correction collar. Ask the dog to take the dumb-bell and start a small obedience routine. When he drops it, apply quick but sharp pops and excitingly ask him to 'take it'.

Once the dog carries the dumb-bell during a short heeling exercise, start short retrieves. Walk through each retrieve with the dog going out only a few feet. Stay close and ready to correct at the moment of refusal. If the dog is reliable after a few sessions, try dropping the lead on the ground, first working close and then moving up to 15 ft (4.5 m).

With older and willing dogs, the compulsive dumb-bell work is learned fast. With sensitive and younger dogs, such work may take more time. One of our dogs, a willing but highly-strung Doberman, caught on to the entire dumb-bell retrieve in less than two weeks.

Since dumb-bell work is stressful, relieve stress-inducing work in the other areas of training. For a few days provide easy tracks, and reduce the amount of defence bite work. Make other obedience work even more playful than normal during this period. Reducing stress in other areas of training maintains the trust already created from past interaction.

Jumping

Often, we run into horror stories about how jumping created physical problems from hip dysplasia to popped knees. It is our experience that the typical Schutzhund jump does not cause physical problems – and we have had our share of physical problems. However, nearly all physical ailments seem to have two sources: genetic or athletic, or some combination of these. If the dog is genetically predisposed to hip, elbow and spinal problems, the weakness will often show up in the working dog. Second, these dogs are athletes, some are super-athletes. This means that they are prone to injury simply because of their speed, agility and drive intensity. It is not rare to watch in horror a star athlete pop a knee whilst chasing down a ball or Kong®. To counter this problem, you may want to reward the dog with a little tug of war with a jute pull instead of using chase toys. Our experience is that running, twisting and turning cause far more injuries than the Schutzhund jump training. If your dog has even normal physical abilities, then with sequential training, he will have little difficulty jumping the regulation 1 m wall.

Teaching the jump begins with clearing an obstacle that is about 5 in (13 cm) in height (even less for a very young pup) with the dog trotting at your side on the leash. Run the dog toward the jump and give the 'jump' command when he reaches it. Upon completion, provide a play period with the chase toy. After a few of these sessions, do the jump, turn about and perform a return jump. Withhold the chase toy until after the return jump. Work at each height level for several sessions, increasing only a little at a time. As long as the dog shows little worry (for instance, refusing to jump) work up to 1 m. If at any time the dog becomes reluctant, decrease the height and work him at this lower level for a few days, then try again. Remember, as with all aspects of obedience, to make a game out of every positive behaviour by throwing the chase toy or playing with a jute pull. Don't forget to add some playful drama and become excited with the exercise yourself.

Once the dog is jumping both out and back (remember to give the 'jump' command with each jump) with you running beside him, now it is time for the dog to start jumping on his own. Lower the hurdle to 2 ft (60 cm) to make the jump easier. With the leash dragging behind the dog, both you and the dog trot toward the hurdle. Upon reaching the hurdle, you stop and eagerly give the 'jump' command. When the dog clears the hurdle on his own, throw the chase toy out in front of him. Don't ask the dog to return over the hurdle during this session.

During the next session, the dog will perform the return jump.

Use a long line attached to the flat collar to guide the return jump. As in the previous session, you trot with the dog toward the hurdle and stop as the dog goes over. When the dog is on the other side, without giving him any time to think about where he is, step to the middle of the jump (on the opposite side from your dog) giving the 'jump' command, thus asking for the return over the hurdle. It is important for the handler to strike the hurdle while simultaneously (and excitingly) giving the 'jump' command. If the dog comes over, good. If he tries to runs around the hurdle, then use the long line, go back to the other side and run beside him giving the 'jump' command. At this point, never let him return without going over the jump.

When the dog is going out and returning over the jump (without the dumb-bell) and is doing the flat retrieve (with the dumb-bell) begin the dumb-bell retrieve over the lowered hurdle. Stand in front of the hurdle and throw the dumb-bell over with the dog at your side and on the long line. Running beside him, give the 'jump' command and, just when he clears the hurdle, give the 'take it' command (the same 'take' command used for the flat retrieve). The first few jumps are almost identical to the flat retrieve, because the dog may be clearing just 6 in (15 cm). If the dog looks good, experiment to see if he needs you at his side at the low height. As he gets familiar with jumping and returning with the dumb-bell, slowly raise the height. When he gets into trouble, always help him and do the next few sessions running beside him.

If you are not already doing so, once he masters retrieving the dumb-bell over the jump and the flat, teach him to go out after the dumb-bell only upon command. Up to this point, he brings the dumb-bell when it leaves your hand. Now command him to stay and throw the dumb-bell. You may need to correct him, but the moment he settles down, command him to bring it and run beside him.

In a separate exercise, begin to teach the dog to pick up the dumb-bell at your feet. When he reaches down for it, step back a little, remembering to provide him some slack on the training collar with your lead. After he picks it up, give the 'come' command and use exactly the same posture as when you want him to finish with a front sit during the come routine. Usually this works quickly. After a few seconds of the front sit, remove the dumb-bell and occasionally do the finish to the side. You are now ready to put it all together with the flat and jump retrieves.

The Send Away

In the true send away, the dog goes straight out from the handler for thirty paces and lies down upon command. A well-trained dog will do this in virtually any direction on any field. The fake send away mirrors the above but the dog goes out to a certain spot, on a familiar field, to search for a toy or food. He does this because that is how trainers teach the send away!

Teaching this exercise began with the toy-chasing reinforcement that went on in other obedience exercises. By now, the dog looks forward to obedience sessions because of all the fun chasing toys. Take his favourite toy and place it at the end of the field – hopefully about 20 ft (6 m) from a fence – with the dog in tow. Let the dog see where you put the toy. Step back a little way and have the dog face the toy, which remains in plain sight. Give the send away command and point in the correct direction. Of course, the dog may not know the command, but anything that you say excitingly should launch him toward the toy. In the beginning, always use the same target spot for the toy as you and your dog back further down the field. Again, just you and your dog move back: do not move the toy because we want the dog to know that the toy is there, even if he cannot see it. Thus, the dog learns to go to the same spot expecting the toy.

Once the dog is going out consistently from a distance of fifty yards, it is time to start teaching him to lie down when he reaches the spot. Do this by starting close to the target spot, essentially beginning again. With the dog a few feet away, place the toy on the spot. Send him on the leash or long line and give the 'down' command when he has the toy. Praise him and throw a second toy, that you have concealed in your pocket. When he comes back to you, give praise and allow him to chew on the toy. While he is chewing, replace the target toy on the spot, still within the dog's vision. Return to the dog and place his toy in your pocket and praise him. When his concentration is off the toy in your pocket, send him to the target toy and command him down when he finds it. When he lies down, throw the second toy over his head. As he becomes familiar to going down on the toy, begin to push the starting point back.

In a separate exercise, place the dog in a stand-stay, walk a short distance, turn and give the 'down' command, throwing the toy over his head upon completion. Although he may not know the stand, simply do a quick and dirty lesson. As he wonders what you're doing, give the 'stay' command. If he sits, gently pull on his leash until he stands, and give the 'stay' command. When he stands for a couple of seconds, give the down command and, of course, immediately throw the chase toy. This process works fast, and you'll have him standing and staying in no time. The behaviour of going down at a distance carries over to the send away down and the 'stand' command carries over to the higher Schutzhund titles. Use the same technique during non-training periods when the dog is simply standing in the yard and you have a toy handy. The goal here is to teach the dog to expect the chase toy when he lies down, upon command, with the handler around 10–15 yards (9–14 m) away.

After a few weeks, the dog is going out fast and going down on the toy. For the next step, it is important always to carry a chase toy, but out of sight. Start the exercise normally, with the target toy on the spot. On the very next repetition, do not place the toy but still go out to do a fake placement for the dog's benefit. With the dog at your side, start a little closer to the target and send him. Jog behind him to remain close. When he reaches the target spot give the 'down' command and a mild correction on the long line if he insists on looking for the toy. This is important: as soon as he lies down, throw the chase toy over his head or off to his side for reinforcement. If you throw the toy anywhere else, he may start creeping toward you after he goes down, anticipating the toy.

On the next repetition, place the toy on the target and run the send away exactly as the dog understands it. That is, he knows that the toy is on the target spot and you just put it there. During following sessions, mix up placing the toy on the target and not placing it, always remembering to throw the toy over his head after he lies down with or without a toy on the target. This is a variation of that old shell game. Again, throwing the chase toy over the dog's head precludes training problems later.

When the dog is going out reliably and lying down, start changing the target areas. Do this by starting close to the new target and placing the toy within sight, and slowly back off for distance. After you have about five of these new targets, ideally a few on different fields, go back to your original target spot. If you plan to do a Schutzhund test on a foreign field, remember to practise the send away on that field before test day.

The Search

Although it is used in protection routines, sending your dog around a blind or object is essentially an obedience function. Therefore we can teach the search on the obedience field and it will carry over during the protection phase.

For most trainers, the search is beautiful to behold. The trained dog, off leash, barely able to restrain himself, lunges toward the empty blind upon release. When he rounds the blind, looking to the handler for direction, we witness that team spirit.

With a willing dog and a lot of prey drive, the search is very easy to teach. If the dog knows the send away, all the better. Start by using an object to hide the toy behind. The object can be anything large enough for a person to hide behind. With your dog a few feet away from the blind, and watching, place the toy in plain sight next to the blind. At this point, don't hide the toy. Give the 'search' command in an excited tone, while simultaneously pointing toward the blind. Your body language and tone should launch him toward the toy. Unlike in the send away, do not command him down when he reaches the toy; instead, call him back. Praise him upon his return and throw the second toy behind you.

Using the same starting position for the dog, begin to move the toy slowly, a few inches at a time, toward the rear of the blind. In no time at all he will be going behind the blind to get the toy. Now you must use some sleight-of-hand. Put the dog in 'stay' and go around the blind, but don't place the toy – leave it in your pocket. The dog thinks the toy is where it always is, behind the blind. Give the 'search' command, then give the call back command when he reaches the blind. If he heads back to you, immediately throw the toy behind you, much like the 'come' routine. However, the dog may insist upon looking for the toy behind the blind. In this event, excitingly get his attention, and throw the toy behind you when he sees that you have what he wants. Next, do two or three searches with the toy behind the blind, then do one sleight-of-hand trick where you keep the toy and send him around the blind only to call him immediately and throw the toy. Work these two methods together until he gets the idea that when you call him, you have the toy. If he slows on going to the blind, then you are going too fast and must place the toy in the blind more often.

After a few weeks of this work, the dog will be going around one blind and coming back. The rest is easy. Place a second blind about 20 ft (6 m) away and put the toy inside. Send him for the toy so that he gets used to the new blind. Then send him for the toy in the first blind a few times. Do this for a few sessions. During the next session, again send him for the toy in the second blind and do the same for the first blind. On the third trip, put the toy in the second blind, walk to the first, then go back to the dog. Send him to the first blind dragging the leash (you may need it on him). As he starts to round the corner on the first blind, call him back as you always do when you have the toy. As he comes back, walk toward the second blind and excitingly point toward it while giving the 'search' command. If he goes over and finds the toy, great! If he comes to you, take his leash and give him a few mild pops while walking him toward the second blind and giving the 'search' command. If at any time he wants to escape you by going toward the blind on his own, let him go. Either way, praise him when he finds the toy in the blind.

Don't demand that he always goes around an empty blind before he gets the toy. Be sure to continue working on the one-blind method, using both blinds, and occasionally ask him to go to the second blind for the toy. Remember to use sleight-of-hand to fool him as to which blind the toy is behind. Do this during training by walking around both blinds before returning to the dog. As he gets better, he will start to cheat by going to the blind that he thinks contains the toy. Anticipate this behaviour and occasionally walk around both blinds but keep the toy, rewarding him with it after he runs both the empty blinds! If he goes to the wrong blind, tell him 'no', call him and give him mild pops in the direction of the correct blind. Soon he will be flying around the empty first blind, all the time knowing that the toy is not there, but listening for you to tell him where it is! We use this method for up to six blinds of various shapes and materials, from fabric and wood blinds to outhouses, to automobiles.

SUMMARY

In summary, break down all obedience routines into sub-routines. It is not necessary to perform the sub-routines in the same order, so you may begin at the end or in the middle on any given session, helping to maintain a high level of interest. Remember to use plenty of verbal, physical and toy rewards, especially when beginning a new learning experience. Remind yourself that your dog is not a machine, so don't demand perfection. What we want is a winning attitude with plenty of drive.

CHAPTER FOUR

Protection

> The police dog of today is the natural development from the herding dog of yesterday. Those peculiarities and aptitudes which enable a dog to succeed in one of these services are equally valuable in the other. The animal's urge to guard and protect, so essential to the preservation of a flock of sheep, is just as valuable in the police service. A patrol dog's first duty is to protect his policeman against assault. Then, too, the trailing ability, by means of which a herder will find a lost lamb, is most valuable to the police dog for he must frequently seek lost objects, missing people and hiding criminals. The transportation of a captured criminal or suspect is quite like the driving of a herd and depends upon similar capacities. A final peculiarity developed by the sheep-herding work which is of value to the police dog is that of the manner of biting so as to hold but not to tear. Especially in subduing older and heavier sheep and rams must the dog be able to employ a forceful grip which, nevertheless, should not seriously injure the animal. Today a police dog will usually overpower a man by using a strong, firm grip and only rarely must it resort to a dangerous, tearing bite.
>
> E. Humphrey, 1934

The Trainer and the Handler

Many new owners of Border Collies react with surprise when learning that other owners of the breed share identical experiences. A frequent narrative begins with the handler and the untrained Collie taking a familiar stroll near a small lake or pond containing several floating ducks or geese. Then one day, the dog suddenly stares at the floating birds with an unusually excited attitude, and to the surprise of his handler, launches into the water. The good-hearted dog first circles the broad-beaked paddlers giving them plenty of space, but comes in close on the far side. Without training, he attempts to 'herd' the birds to shore!

From many similar anecdotes about other breeds, we understand that the basic herding mentality appears innate in good working dogs. This herding predisposition is a barometer of a breed's willingness to work. However, while we may have a natural working dog, without training a dog will not help us against a determined human attack. Of the many hundreds of dogs tested for protection work, we have yet to come across our first dog able to bite and hold a serious human attacker without training.

In light of this, it is astounding to us that many dog show professionals and lay people question the validity of training for protection. This view incorporates the fantasy that the untrained family pet will naturally protect against attack, regardless of personality or genetic background. Interestingly, this may very well be true if the 'attacker' is running away, but no one needs help against a repentant or fleeing robber! Rather we need help against the determined attacker who shows no fear of a dog – or of anything else for that matter.

It is instinctive for domestic dogs to respect people. It is instinctive for nearly all other animals to fear and avoid human beings. Since the dog is most likely related to the wolf, we are working against at least two genetic traits that instruct the dog not to bite people. For these reasons alone, the good working dog must have proper training to identify and protect against the dangerous human assailant, while simultaneously remaining impartial in the company of regular people.

There *are* signs that certain biting traits are innate, therefore genetic. However, it is important to recall that the environment does influence genetic predispositions. To a certain degree, it is true that courage, or 'gameness', is apparent in the five-week-old pup. Yet, even the potentially toughest dog will become submissive with incompetent training, both formal and informal. Proper training enhances inherent potential and overall stability by teaching the dog several important behaviours: a courageous defensive attack, obedience to the handler, concentration on task (taught through tracking), and remaining unruffled around people.

Without training, it is exceedingly difficult for a dog to defend his owner against a resolute attacker. Even wild wolves withhold from biting people, mostly from overwhelming fear. But for both dogs and tamed wolves, the entire human species becomes, more or less, a part of their 'pack'. This innate social trait produces an animal who will live happily with people, but makes ongoing protection training mandatory.

While the social drive inhibits the dog from biting members of the pack with higher status (even an attacking human), it provides trainers with the psychological tool necessary to work closely with the dog. The trick is to get the social drive to work *for* the trainer, rather than against. The trainer/handler does this by becoming the dog's alpha leader, rather than the master. Once the dog understands that his handler is also his leader, the size of the human pack narrows considerably in the mind of the dog. By contrast, the master/dog relationship results in confusion, over-submissiveness, robotic training responses lacking independent thinking, and the tendency to view all people as pack members.

The single training attitude most likely to create the master/dog relationship is severe over-correction. Severe treatment forces the dog to view the handler as the 'master' rather than the leader. Apparently, over-corrections tend to enhance the social drive and, in the worse case, result in over-submissiveness. Unfortunately, it takes very little to produce the master/dog relationship. In most households, motivated by fear and misunderstanding, family members systematically teach the pup to become non-aggressive in all activities. Combine this schooling with the dog's natural inhibition toward biting pack members (including people), and you have a dog trained not to bite and therefore, a dog trained not to help against a determined personal attack. However, despite these facts, films continue to feed the myth that 'when push comes to shove', the family pet will protect.

Transition of Training Standards

Training the dog in bite work appears confusing and mystical to both the newly initiated and often to the experienced, but uninformed, handler. This is because training clubs, the very source of most dog education, tend to be without substance. Confusion all too often occurs today even in established dog clubs as protection training becomes more and more embraced by the middle class. During the 1920s, and continuing to the present day, these wealthy, competitive people generally re-defined the peasant art of dog training into a palatable 'sport'.

With these new 'sporting' people characterizing an egotistical investment in dog training, the general public responded and market pressures were brought to bear on working dog breeders for changes that reflected a superficial lifestyle. These lay people desired for themselves the image of a German Shepherd owner, but were unable or unwilling to commit to the necessary training. Therefore, breeders began programmes which combined low drives with a new standard of 'beauty'. In very little time, breeders produced dogs whom even the untrained and unteachable may handle. The result we see today is dogs plagued with serious hip, elbow and spinal problems and far less gameness compared to dogs of the early twentieth century.

In recent years, public opinion in Germany, the birthplace of the modern working dog, appears to be growing negative toward protection training. Responding to this pressure, Schutzhund clubs incorporated the 'B' title. This title, also known as the 'companion title', attempted to appease the public by showing that the dog passed several tests of socialization and obedience. Next, Schutzhund officials replaced the reed stick with a heavier, but showingly padded stick. With public pressure unrelenting, Schutzhund officials changed the courage test. The helper no longer runs away from the dog (the supposed source of concern) then turns to attack, but runs only toward the dog for the attack. Of course, no matter how many changes Schutzhund officials make, public opinion will not change through appeasement, but only through education.

Any education or formal training standard must show that the balanced protection dog is not out of control, or some savage beast, but a solid animal who is an asset to the public and a lesser danger than the untrained dog. Education must show that without solid drive theory, a dog becomes badly trained. Informative education about proper dog training techniques will help the public to understand that the protection dog is beneficial to have nearby, and is only dangerous to attackers.

However, as in most situations, there are two viewpoints of formal standardized training. While standardized training may force trainers to educate the public that trainers are accountable for training excellent dogs, the negative side is that of bureaucratic control and compulsion, which stifles creativity and the training spirit.

The Training Plan

For teaching purposes, it is important to understand the parameters of incompetent training – if only to know what to avoid. The underlying cause of incompetent training is the general lack of respect and understanding for everyone concerned: the dog, the handler, general onlookers and even the self. We often observe trainers entering the training field only to regress and worry about what others are thinking, rather than adjusting training strategies to changing behaviour. This often occurs even in the case of the well-versed (those with the ability to articulate several dog training theories) and best-intentioned trainers. These so-called trainers learned long ago that the cultivation of human perception enhances the self-image – and perhaps the wallet as well. To such people, training becomes secondary to image maintenance, regardless of what they say before entering and after leaving the training field.

The single most common training error is pushing the dog in defence work whilst ignoring all the warning signs. Although the dog is unable to bite during defence, the trainer pushes ahead with teaching the out, or release; moves ahead with all of the decoy's posturing for advanced dogs; hits with the stick; asks the dog to bite hidden sleeves or the body suit; and works the dog at a distance from the handler. Often, bizarre and more obvious errors occur, of which handlers must be aware.

We recall the case of a trainer striking a dog several times with the stick after being told that the dog was without stick training. The trainer mentioned that he 'wanted the dog's respect'. Of course, the dog became stick shy. In another stick incident, when the handler asked the trainer why he struck his dog severely for a total of six times, the trainer responded 'It's a Schutzhund dog, isn't it?' Another trainer became frustrated and proceeded to scream in German at the dog. He said later that he 'was trying to teach the dog'. We are not very sure about this training strategy, but certainly noted that the novice handlers present were very impressed!

In another incident, after being told by the handler that the dog was slowing during the courage test, the trainer insisted on doing a courage test so that he could see how slow 'slow' was.

One more case (among the many). We worked for months to get a dog to hold the decoy closely and intensely, and our efforts paid off. The handler felt that the dog was ready for trial, so we recommended that he go to several trainers in the area and proof the dog with new decoys. On the new field the dog charged into the blind, but ran squarely into the decoy's kick. Running into the kick was to teach the dog to 'respect the trainer'. The dog fell back to his former behaviour of holding decoys about four feet away. It took nearly five weeks to teach the dog to hold close again.

These examples highlight the fact that other trainers and decoys may not rely upon trial behaviours or training theories that the handler may take for granted. Therefore, it is most important to preplan nearly every move with a new decoy. We recommend to go over the lesson plan by telephone first and then again at the training field. The time to iron out differences in both theory and personality is when the dog is in the crate, rather than on the field.

Bite Theory

In theory, there are two basic bite drives (behaviour traits or personality attitudes) of the working dog: prey and defence. Trainers who fail to know which drive the dog uses during a bite are incompetent, for this is pivotal knowledge for effective training. Any training programme built upon an incorrect foundation, or one wrongly guessed, will fail at some point if allowed to continue.

Related to this, the next mistake that trainers frequently commit is the failure to understand which drive (prey or defence) is stronger in a particular dog. When trainers and handlers make these mistakes, they commit what we call a 'failure to read the dog'.

The misread dog becomes bombarded with training techniques that impede progress over the long term, although the dog may look very good for a few months. We once saw a misread dog pass the Schutzhund I test, although this is rare. Later, the dog's bite deteriorated in training for the next title. Without the use of correct training fundamentals, future progress will break down.

Take, for example, the high defence dog misread as a predominantly prey dog. If this dog fails to learn the out or release, during the long months of prey-bite training, although he progresses in other areas, he will not learn the out during defence-bite training without severe measures such as electric collars, or wrestling with the dog on the sleeve for fifteen to twenty minutes waiting for lactic acid build-up. The result is a hard fighting dog, but one out of control. We often see many such dogs unable to release without the electric collar: these are useless to us.

This leads us to another difficult area; the application of training techniques. All training techniques must incorporate both handler and dog, and take into consideration the degree of rapport existing between them. If, in the worst case, the dog does not trust his handler, the best of trainers and techniques will amount to nothing. Without trust, any correction equates to an attack by the handler! The same is true if the dog feels he is alpha over the handler. Dogs with such problems are not ready for serious training – much less bite work – since they are unable to work with the handler.

Poor training techniques may also be applied to the correctly read dog. For example, instead of using the training collar to teach the dog that he must release from the sleeve, he is 'flanked'. 'Flanking' is pinching the sensitive skin near the belly in front of the rear leg. In one situation, this method was used so often that the rapport between the handler and dog disappeared. The dog felt that the handler was attacking him, so he attacked his handler. At this point the handler decided to sell the dog.

Another example is the novice dog who will not track because of confusion. The correct technique in this case is to pack up and go home and slightly decrease the dog's food before tracking again: a little hunger may focus his attention. For the novice dog with motivation problems, incorrect handler reactions are to apply training collar pressure; to use less bait on the track; to increase the number of distracting people in the area; to add confusing cross-tracks, and to add even more articles. In short, this type of trainer expects the dog to learn on a harder track, despite the obvious difficulty with an easier track. Such training has no basis in behavioural theory.

Back on the protection field, another example of correct reading but incorrect technique may occur when trying to set the bite on the sleeve. Normally this happens on the back-tie or the long line. The trainer, with the dog on the sleeve, pulls against the back-tie, forcing the dog to instinctively grip harder. This is a good technique. The incorrect method occurs off-line and uses the dog's bodyweight in a whipping motion. The handler releases the dog to attack the trainer for a mini-test of courage. The trainer slightly sidesteps the dog and uses the dog's bodyweight to set the bite. The problem is that the novice dog's body whips past the trainer and snaps taut. For the novice dog, beside adding an unnecessary defence attitude which is difficult to fine-tune, this method also places stress upon jaw muscles, head, neck and spine, thereby risking injury. Whether injured or not, the bite does indeed set, but why gamble with injury and unnecessary stress? Where safer techniques exist for the same goal, techniques that may cause injury or soreness are always unnecessary.

Training Competence

Competent handlers record observed behaviours and incorporate that knowledge into a lesson plan with goals and objectives. A training plan is not what the trainer or handler wistfully feels or believes, but is based upon accurate training theory and upon where the dog is behaviourally and psychologically at any given point. Any such plan must come from the competent handler, who will know the dog better than anyone. The trainer or helper must agree to the plan before the dog steps onto the training field. Most importantly, the plan does not use trial exercises as goals. Training goals incorporate techniques that build a strong dog with a winning attitude. This may mean that the attack on handler heeling routine is broken into five sections, with each section ending with bite work.

Without lesson plans, trainers work from memory, and we know that memory is less than precise. Working from faulty memory is a serious hindrance to training progress, and is tantamount to training with little or no thought. Building the dog 'from the seat of the pants' or from feeling where the dog is at, and not individually analysing each dog on the amount of time spent on process and techniques, is at best mediocre practice, and at worst, a training disaster.

Without a training plan, seat-of-the-pants trainers immediately minimize everything the handler mentions about the dog, because any new information forces different thought processes. If the handler explains that the dog is high in defence, and needs work only in prey, the trainer will exacerbate the problem by working the dog in defence 'to see where he's at'. One reason for this is that the trainer cannot remember the point the dog has reached in the training process because of failure to keep records of past training sessions. Another reason, right or wrong, is that the trainer fails to trust the handler's observation. Regardless of the trainer's opinion of the handler, the prudent trainer will always select the option that provides less stress for the dog. Over several sessions, the trainer creates a baseline recording of the dog's performance. The behavioural baseline is the correct starting point from which to begin working in defence or to provide more defence pressure.

In summary, the lesson plan is necessary, and it must incorporate the dog's basic drive orientation (behavioural baseline); the exact behaviours of both the handler and helper; possible outcomes of various techniques, and the resultant alternative plan.

The Grip: or How to Evaluate a Trainer

The goal of protection training is the powerful bite under defence pressure, combined with handler control. With bone-crushing strength, a strong bite grips the sleeve with the entire mouth. The dog may appear calm, or be fighting the decoy with his front legs and body. When the full bite actually occurs during defence pressure by the decoy, we note effective bite training. This only happens in defence work that does not create too much stress.

On the other hand, if we are considering a dog with a good genetic background,[1] the poorly trained dog worries defensively, exhibiting behaviour such as growling, half- or even quarter-grips, tearing, chewing, backing off the sleeve, weak or timid biting, warning with the show of teeth and – in extreme cases – running away. To the novice, these displays of weakness (except the last) appear powerful. After all, films forever depict the snarling, growling dog as a serious force. However, any decoy will tell you that the poorly trained dog must be watched to be certain that he is on the sleeve, since the dog's bite pressure is so weak that the decoy can't feel any grip, even though the dog may look and sound tough.

Other stress-related behaviour that may occur while the dog is either on or off the sleeve are: avoiding eye contact and avoiding the helper's front by moving to the side. Another problem of the dog displaying high defence is a refusal to comply with handler commands. This occurs because he is not fighting with a joyful, serious and confident attitude, but from too much fear.

Another indication of poor training is when we see a novice dog biting poorly because of too much defence work, but biting hard and full after a few weeks off from training. The novice trainer misreads this observation as proof that the dog responded to 'rest'. This is not the case. The dog is biting from a genetic residue of courage. As stated elsewhere, even an alpha dog will gradually become a submissive urinater given constant poor handling and training. In the case just mentioned, the dog found what he needed

[1]With some dogs of certain breeds, it is nearly impossible for them to learn to fight an attacking human, hence the use of the term 'good genetic background'.

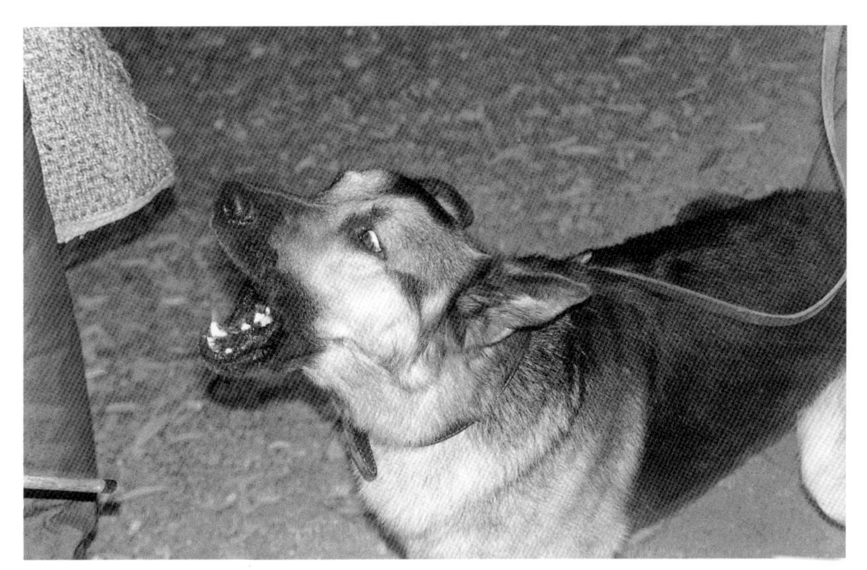

Avoiding eye contact with the decoy: sleeve fixation.

in other areas of training, or in the home situation. Sadly, dogs in this training situation soon revert to their pre-learned modes of stress-biting weaknesses, eventually getting so bad that the dog runs away or bites so weakly that the trainer is compelled to use a puppy sleeve to get any bite at all. Ignoring high defence signs is essentially training the dog how not to bite.

There is another curious behaviour displayed by the predominately prey dog working too high in defence: he may show avoidance of the decoy by focusing on the sleeve (commonly known as being 'sleeve happy'). This will not occur in the predominately defence dog, for he will want only the decoy.[2] Oddly, both will be out of handler control if worked too high in defence. That is, neither dog will release from the sleeve. However, in the former case (a predominately prey dog overworked in defence), if he is slipped the sleeve, he will concentrate upon the sleeve as a means of avoiding the decoy, whom he fears.

The second way of producing a sleeve-happy dog is simply incomplete training. This works as follows: although the prey and defence

[2]Defence dogs are also poor retrievers; and they dislike carrying the sleeve. However, they have a greater alert zone than prey dogs and are unlikely to develop serious avoidance problems.

Decoy feigning fear; a prey behaviour.

'Fearful' decoy and supporting fence for young dog.

Frontal decoy posture; defence position.

drives may be balanced in the properly trained advanced dog, the dog did not receive civil agitation, body suit or hidden sleeve experience. Therefore, the dog only knows how to bite a sleeve. Yet it takes very, very little to teach the properly trained advanced dog to bite a decoy wearing a body suit, or the hidden sleeve. Usually all that is necessary is for the familiar decoy to appear wearing the hidden sleeve or the body suit, and the handler to give the 'bite' command. The dog performs because everything is in context – with the exception of the missing sleeve.

Balancing Prey and Defence

Prey and defence drives tend to both help and complicate the best trainer's programme. This is because the amount of drive a particular dog may have depends upon both genetic and environmental determinants. Some are 'defence' dogs who will not avoid the fight, yet show all the bite characteristics of weakness. The 'prey' dogs have a powerful bite and a joyful attitude, yet with poor defence training they will struggle with avoidance behaviours. Further, as stated earlier, prey dogs who lack the defence attitude become lost without the sleeve. For the prey dog, the sleeve is essentially a toy. However, for the defence dog, the sleeve is the nearest part of the decoy to bite. If the decoy tossed the sleeve aside, the defence dog would have no trouble biting his leg, arm or back.

The training goal for any working dog is to balance the drives to obtain a fighting, powerful bite, with accompanying control. In the case of the prey dog, he learns not to avoid but to overcome defence pressure, while the defence dog learns to bite harder, fuller and to remain calm and under handler control.

The dog who is too high in prey characteristics may have behavioural indicators of this beside avoidance. Such dogs are good retrievers and love to carry the rag or sleeve. Barking is often weak or less intense, almost as if barking for bait or food. While some trainers dislike working with these heavily prey-oriented dogs, other trainers appreciate them because they enjoy working on balancing the drives to produce fine protection and competition dogs. Prey dogs are amenable to training and are handler-sensitive, while defence dogs need experienced handlers and a great deal of firmness. Nevertheless, with complete training and depending upon the individual dog, both personality traits can produce a very, very strong dog who is under complete handler control.

To avoid confusion at this point, let us explain that it is the high defence *behaviour* that is undesirable, not the defence attitude. The defence attitude is the most important component of the protection dog's psychological orientation, for it is this that prompts the protection of the handler when under determined attack. Competent trainers point out that, while the defence attitude has intensity and

Full defence attack: this dog is ready.

violence, defence is necessary in order to balance the drives. As stated above, the defence dog without drive balance will not calm down enough for handler control. With the introduction of prey work, and a few other calming techniques discussed later, the defence dog will learn to switch to prey drive for controllability. Again, the key to training is to balance the two drives.

To test the quality of the balance of drives at any particular organization is not difficult. If the advanced dogs, under defence pressure, are biting full and hard whilst remaining under control, and are simultaneously giving the decoy a good fight, you are observing good bite training. If you witness anything less, then you know that training failures exist.

Once on the field, the training programme depends upon the helper (decoy) for success or failure. With the novice dog, it doesn't take very much for the inexperienced decoy to set training back several months. The power that the helper has to raise defence beyond tolerance with eye contact alone is phenomenal. It is most important for the helper working on defence to break eye contact with the dog, or shift into prey moves, before the dog looks away. This (quite subtly in the case of the former), gives the dog a 'win' and strengthens confidence with little decoy effort. However, the opposite may occur with the poor helper who is not self-aware. Such a helper maintains eye contact without being aware of it, and wonders why the dog grows higher in defence even though supposedly working prey. The experienced decoy notes that if the dog shows high defence behaviours, then the helper is actually working in defence, regardless of intention or belief. However, the inexperienced decoy nearly always blames the genetic background of the dog for training setbacks.

Weak, quarter-grip bite.

Extremely timid bite.

A solid, full bite

The technique the effective decoy uses to obtain the correct fighting attitude is to work the intermediate and advanced dog higher and higher in defence without losing the power of the prey bite. The definition of the 'hard' dog is one who has the full, powerful bite alongside the extreme intensity of the defence attitude.

A secondary training problem related to the above, but with a difference, is pushing the dog before he is ready. The behavioural sign for pushing the dog is the same as high defence. The essence of 'pushing' is carrying on with defence work despite biting or releasing problems. Thus the trainer continues to teach the dog other parts of the defence curriculum, for instance, advanced holds (such as finding and holding or biting a hidden decoy in building searches), car searches, and natural field searches. Across the spectrum, pushed dogs are uncontrollable (in that they are unable to release); they bite at will, or show other classic avoidance behaviour. Trainers who push dogs are either unable to get the sense of dog training, or they pray for some sort of miracle. Usually they want a miracle dog, who will do the right thing no matter what the trainer does.

We may define drives as 'attitudes', or 'personality traits'. In the protection dog with incomplete, or incompetent training, one attitude will outweigh the other. During training, the prey dog may switch to high defence behaviour (avoidance) in a matter of seconds. At the very centre of these attitudes is the emotion that dictates fight or flight. The effective decoy must anticipate when to induce and when to relieve pressure on the novice dog. If the training design calls for the young dog to win, confidence and the fight response strengthen. The more the novice dog fails to win, the higher defence rises, and the more likely it is that weak biting, uncontrollability or flight may occur. Therefore, we must balance the two drives under consideration. The trick is to get the serious nature of the defence attitude high, while maintaining control and the powerful bite. After the pup reaches the age of about twelve to fourteen months, training is made serious with the introduction of decoy behaviours designed to bring out the defence drive in the dog. If defence training does not occur, then the dog works below potential, with the sleeve remaining a toy and protection training simply an obedience game. This dog cannot be counted upon to protect.

It is crucial that both the trainer and the handler read the dog correctly once defence training commences. At this point, what is done determines the future of a service dog. The problem is that new handlers seem predisposed to complacency. Both new and experienced handlers often place irrational trust in the trainer and the choice of training direction. The typical verbal expression of this mental line is, 'I'll do whatever the trainer says'. Psychological literature calls this human predisposition 'transference'. Essentially, the trainer becomes a parent. These handlers are not weak people; the majority being characteristically stiff-necked in other aspects of their lives. The transference syndrome occurs in protection dog training because of the primal fear of teeth. Since our first fears occur during early childhood, the handler unconsciously makes the connection and does what a child would do, that is, searches for a parent – in this case, the trainer.

The new handler must overcome this tendency with logical, reasoned study of the working dog, and thus become competent. A competent handler will not approach training as another item to buy (that is, paying the trainer's fee) without further psychological research and time investment. Competent handlers do their own research and use the trainer for guidance. Eventually, the handler takes over the training and learns to work directly with the decoy.

Some may ask how the handler can become the trainer, but essentially every handler is a trainer. The competent handler, like any good parent, knows the dog better than anyone, including the trainer. The alert and critical handler has a clearer picture of the lessons mastered and the dog's progress during any training session. The reason for this is that the handler may have one dog, but the trainer works with far more. Most bite work and related training takes weeks, if not months or years, making record-keeping or a photographic memory essential. Since record-keeping by the trainer is unlikely, the handler can fill in. Therefore, it is essential that the training team should include the handler. Like any team, lines of communication must remain open before, during and after training sessions. A major communication objective of the training team is to teach the handler to become a trainer. In the world of working dogs, hiding training theory behind techniques is not only improper, but disrupts the team and the overall training process.

The Art of Drive Work

An important aspect of bite work is the helper, or decoy. The helper, whether working prey or defence, must be conscious of eye contact, body position, and sleeve and stick position. During prey work there is little or no eye contact; the sleeve moves from side to side either by swinging (for the advanced dogs) or by the helper jogging along an arc in front of the dog. Once the dog is on the sleeve, the decoy continues to work prey by first dragging the dog, then releasing the sleeve for the carry and win.

The helper enhances prey work by presenting the side of the body to the dog. For some young dogs, it may be necessary for the helper to crouch down, kneel, or lie upon the ground to bring out the prey bite and to avoid high defence worry. We know of one case where the handler occasionally took the sleeve and taught his dog to bite hard. This team went on to take 'High In Trial' at a Schutzhund contest less than six months later. In another case, the helper found that the young dog would at first bite only when he backed up to the dog and handler.

Conversely, to work defence, the helper *slowly* introduces opposite behaviours to the dog. The decoy sequentially introduces the frontal position, then eye contact, strokes with the stick, drives, runs toward the dog, shouts, asks for the hold and bark, civil agitation, asks the handler for the 'out' command, and allows the dog to carry less. Between defence posturing, the decoy provides the dog with prey bites to maintain confidence. If the dog is biting well, the decoy begins to increase the time element to each of the above, while still giving occasional prey bites for relief. The true essence of teaching bite work is producing a dog with the experience necessary to instil a sense of confidence.

As mentioned earlier, the young dog experiences only prey work, but once this stage ends, bite work must have both drives worked.

Again, the helper slowly introduces defence work, often returning to prey work to reduce pressure and maintain the bite. Defence work is not a step-by-step process, but more a case of one step forward and two steps back. Therefore, every two or three sessions, the defence pressure rises slightly. The fourth session may be nearly all prey work. This gives the young dog a break and maintains a progressing level of confidence.

In a very real way, the essence of 'reading' a dog is to allow the dog to dictate how much pressure you should apply. Competent trainers will always state that the good dog trains himself, and good decoys assert that they are just there to follow the dog's instructions.

Teaching Protection

Even if we find a trainer who understands drive theory and attempts to balance the dog's attitudes, we often come across a training problem arising from trying to teach the dog through the weaker drive. When it comes to drive work, 'practice makes perfect' is not true. In the novice prey dog, if defence is weak, then working only defence will make him weaker to the point of running away. This observation harmonizes with the decoy correctly switching into prey moves at the instant of detecting anxiety when working defence. On the other hand, if the decoy works the novice defence dog only in defence, we soon have a dog beyond handler control.

If the prey drive is dominant, then work through prey techniques and slowly introduce defensive pressure once the pup reaches twelve to fourteen months of age. When the dog exhibits any symptoms of high defence, we back off defensive pressure and launch prey techniques. When he bites consistently full, we reintroduce defence pressure. The idea is to switch between drives, giving the dog plenty of wins in the early stages. These shifting techniques start in the strong drive, whether prey or defence, and shift to the weaker. By allowing the dog to win in the weak drive, he gains confidence, which strengthens the weaker drive. In time, the two drives become balanced and strong.

Take, for example, the helper who works closer and closer to the prey dog to build defence. The instant the dog shows any sign of high defence symptoms, the helper must reduce pressure by adopting prey tactics. It is also important to note the distance between the helper and dog at which signs of defensive worry occur. During the next session, the helper switches to prey tactics at the point in time and distance where the dog showed anxiety in the past. It is important to shift into prey tactics *before* the dog shifts into worry. Assuming a dog is biting well, the helper can slightly push the anxiety distance during the next session, switching to prey tactics just before anticipating worry. To put it another way, we simply push the dog's 'space' a few inches, then shift to prey tactics. Thus we pressure the dog slightly, only to take the pressure off before worry develops, resulting in the dog gaining confidence. This is what we call teaching the dog how to bite.

Again, working the dog through his weaker drive, to 'become stronger', is another way to ruin potential by teaching the dog *not* to bite or to become out of control, depending upon the fundamental drive of the dog. For example, consider the trainer working the weaker drive, in this case, defence in the prey dog, despite a display of high defence worry (too high defence). The result will be lack of control, weak biting, or the dog running away under pressure.

The defence dog who shows very little prey drive is also taught through his drive strength, reverting to prey techniques only for a calming effect. Calming the defence dog provides control and a powerful bite. Therefore, the decoy works this dog in the same fashion as the prey dog, but for different reasons. Both dogs receive prey moves to reduce anxiety. However, the novice prey dog receives prey moves to keep him engaging the helper, but the more advanced defence dog receives prey moves immediately after defence work to maintain control and the full bite.

Prey Biting for Beginners

At this point, it is a good idea to review some information from the chapter on pups (Chapter 2). This helps to maintain continuity between teaching prey biting and the beginning of teaching defence biting, with its attending defence behaviours.

If the twelve-week-old pup is biting a rag or towel at home, begin decoy biting using a clean burlap sack. The decoy merely plays tug of war, remembering to always let the pup win. Allow him to carry the rag around the yard until he lets it go, only to start the game again. If he is familiar with the leash, rag play and let him win, then jog him in the yard. While jogging, don't allow him to lower his head to chew on the rag or re-bite. If he tries to drop and chew the sack, gently pull him along (with the leash on the flat collar) for a few feet until the rag falls and he is unable to reach the new toy.

It is not unusual to find a pup who drops the rag immediately after the win and stands over it in a guarding position. Gently have fun with the pup and try timidly to steal the rag. If he tries to bite, the decoy must run away in mock fear. We always play this game with new pups, often taking small baby nips for our efforts.

As the pup bites stronger, pull a little harder on the rag and begin to make him jump for the bite. Once he is on the rag, get down to his level and pull his body onto yours, stroke him with your free hand and lightly push him away. If the pup has no problem with a hand touching him while he is on the bite, now is the time to imprint the acceptance of sticks. Do this by very gently stroking his sides and back while he is on the bite. Let him win the rag for his courage, being certain to stop the rag game before the puppy tires.

Continue to watch him closely to see how long he holds the rag after he wins. Once you get the approximate time, begin the 'out' imprinting by coaxing him with the command at about the time when he normally drops the rag. Do not correct the pup, and do not touch the rag if he fights for control. If he drops the rag, reward him with an immediate tug game. Practice this 'out' style with his toys as well.

For the more timid pup who needs more maturity, allow him to watch the older dogs (especially the loud barkers) biting the sleeve, when back-tied on the flat collar. After several sessions of doing very little (for the typical pup), the young dog will start barking weakly at other dogs and begin pulling on the lead. Allow the pup to pull you a few feet. During the next few sessions, as he reacts more strongly, put more distance between him and the advanced dog.

Carrying a slipped sleeve: prey move.

Once the pup reacts strongly to the advanced dog or helper, the helper begins rag work from a distance, using a barely audible hissing sound. If the pup barks even once, the helper must turn and run in mock fright. If the pup is slightly timid, allow the helper to approach with a rag tied to a 6 ft (2 m) lead, dragging it past the pup's nose. Some pups respond easily to the rag when it is far from the helper.

Response to the helper work may be higher with some pups than others, depending upon experience, prior home training and everyday conditioning. Here is a method often used to get less experienced pups to respond. Place all the pups in a large circle around the helper. As the helper runs by with the enticing rag, offering and giving bites, some slower pups become excited. (Of course, the helper simply runs by the pups on an arc, never directly *at* a pup.)

After a few months of rag work, the pup will be biting strongly. Around ten months of age, introduce a puppy sleeve[3] in the middle of a rag session by enticing him with the rag, only to place it on the puppy sleeve at the same moment as offering the bite. Once he bites the sleeve, it is slipped off the arm for the win (exactly as the dropped rag is won). For the next few sessions, depending upon the dog, alternate between sleeve and rag.

[3]Some pups are able to bite a regular sleeve at six months. Always adjust training to fit the dog.

Once the pup is prey-biting the sleeve nicely, start to do runaway bites on the long line for short distances. At first slip the sleeve, then let him fight it by dragging him a bit. Slowly work up to long runaways on leash. This entire process begins again with off-line runaways, both short and distant.

Runaway bite: prey move.

The dog, at this point, is around a year old. He is feeling confident with prey biting and runaways, so we are ready for defence training.

With the dog on the back-tie, and the handler at his side, the sleeve helper works prey, shifting to the defence posturing discussed earlier (see page 110), and then back to prey before the dog gets anxious. If the dog shows any sign of defence in these early stages, the helper must slip into prey moves to take the pressure off. As when teaching prey biting, during the initial stages of defence work the helper slips the sleeve often for the win. This is crucial when the dog is making good progress in defence: the slipped sleeve is another level of reinforcement.

Work the dog between prey and defence in this way for the next few months, or until he is confidently biting hard and full under pressure. The handler offers some verbal praise during prey moves, but remains silent during defence moves. Defence in the dog is not a pack trait, but an individual trait. This attitude relies upon the

Long line runaway.

dog's character and heart; therefore the handler remains silent as the dog fights the posturing sleeve helper and hangs onto the sleeve during intense drives. The helper must build the dog's confidence by never driving and fighting more than the dog can safely tolerate. Such a helper provides confidence by occasionally slipping the sleeve or performing prey moves while on the sleeve. (Again, during a prey drag, the helper, with back toward the dog, pulls the dog along on the sleeve.)

Hold, Bark and Out

The Schutzhund trial requires the dog to bark forcefully only inches from the motionless decoy. This is the 'hold and bark'. Introduce this defence exercise when the dog does long line work and defence biting is progressing. At first, while attached to the line, the handler gives the 'search' command as the helper stands passively a few inches from the barking dog, giving a bite after several barks. This is the beginning of the hold. Do this while slowly releasing line pressure from the collar. The helper gives the bite after one or two barks and no line pressure. After a few sessions, measure 5–6 ft (1.7 m) of line, attach it to the flat collar, and release the dog with the 'search' command. The handler must take up the slack just before the dog reaches the quiet helper. With novice dogs, some helpers put the sleeve behind them at the beginning of this procedure.

For the difficult dog, there is a variation of the above. If, after several sessions of performing the hold technique using the flat collar, little progress occurs, measure 5–6 ft (1.7 m) from the helper and attach the line to the training collar. Release the dog with the 'search' command *easing* him with the line when he reaches the helper. Continue with the bark, loose line, and bite procedure. After a few of these short distance easings with the training collar, give a sharper pop, if needed, when he reaches the helper. This should be enough to get his attention and to demand the performance of what he has already learned.

As the dog learns, work on the following points one at a time, moving on only with progress.

The beginning hold: note long line pressure.

1. Gradually increase the distance between the helper and dog before releasing him with the 'search' command when working on holds (this re-accustoms the dog to work apart from the handler).
2. Begin working on holds with the helper at first standing outside the blind. Over the next few sessions have the helper's position move gradually from the side of the blind to the inside of the blind for the hold and bark. For the novice dog, the helper's position does not change during a session.
3. The next step is the off-line hold and bark. Do the off-line work only when on-line holds are going well. Remember to start the routine at the simple level. Therefore, start with the helper fairly close, say 4–6 ft (1.2–1.8 m).

There are two things to keep in mind about the hold and bark. First, it is a defence activity, therefore progress slowly over many sessions. It is difficult to give a timescale as some dogs progress quickly, while others, like Dobermans and Rottweilers, progress slowly because they mature more slowly. What is 'slow'? Recall all the behaviours that identify the high defence frame of mind. When the dog displays this problem, it is essential to relieve stress with prey moves and bites for a session or two. Even if the dog is looking good in defence, it is always advisable to let the novice carry the sleeve to the automobile for the win at the end of the session. Again, for many dogs, even if they are looking good in defence, it may be a good idea to provide a couple of prey bites in the middle of defence work. If at any time there is a lack of spirit, or high defence signs occur during holds, return to the back-tie or long line and continue with drive development, adding lots of sleeve slips.

Hold and bark training problems occur when inexperienced trainers attach the long line to the training collar, measure 30 ft (9 m) from the standing helper, and release the dog with the 'search' command. When the dog reaches the helper, the pinch collar brings him to a painful stop. This method may create problems of avoidance of the helper or the blind.

Whenever the dog wins the sleeve and runs a circle, the drive lowers. This is the time to start work on teaching the 'out', if defence work is progressing. (Normally, teaching the 'out' begins at this point – but not always. For the dog identified with a defence personality at a young age, it may be taught during prey biting.[4]) The helper slips the sleeve, which the dog carries easily. The handler jogs the dog in a circle to calm him and to keep the dog from dropping the sleeve and chewing it. At this point, the handler gives the 'out' command. If he doesn't release, the handler again jogs him in a circle and repeats the command after halting. If he doesn't release at this point, the dog will try to pin the sleeve to the ground and chew. The handler prevents this by simply holding the dog's head up with the leash.

An alternative to jogging the dog is to take him by the protection collar (the flat collar), lift his front feet off the ground, and give the 'out' command. Both methods build upon the toy retrieval release already taught. However slowly it happens, once

[4]The 'out' command is not totally new to the dog, for he has learned to release toys.

the dog consistently performs the release under these conditions, give a mild pop to the training collar to quicken the release.

Teaching the 'out' on the slipped sleeve sets up for the behaviour without the slip. Combined with a mild training collar pop if necessary, the dog will perform the release just as he learned with the slipped sleeve. After the release, immediately reward the dog with a prey bite, prey drag and the slip.

When correcting the dog for the 'out' without the sleeve slip, stand behind the helper and pop the leash toward yourself. The effect is correcting toward the sleeve. This reduces confusion caused by past training on the back-tie. Remember that the dog spent hours pulling on the back-tie or long line when going after the bite. Correcting on the training collar in the same direction as the back-tie pull slows progress for the novice dog. Once the dog releases the decoy, provide an immediate re-bite and a sleeve slip for the win.

Even after the dog has learned the release, good defence training and confidence building often cause the good dog to ignore the 'out' command. Remember the one step forward and two steps back training rule? Release the sleeve and run him in a circle to lower his drive and again give the 'out' command, but with a correction. On the following bite, the handler, with a leash on the training collar, steps behind the quiet helper while giving the 'out' command with a simultaneous firm correction. The dog will come off. Remember, although the dog himself may be releasing nicely, don't command an 'out' on every bite. Continue releasing the sleeve every few bites for the win.

Once the dog releases the sleeve, he may begin to re-bite through high drive. Instead of using the correction collar, first calm the dog after he releases by talking, stroking his sides, or both. When he channels his drive into powerful barking, (something he learned when on the back-tie or long line) the helper immediately gives the bite. The dog does not get another bite without barking, and if he is barking he is not trying to re-bite, therefore the bark is an important drive deflection tool. At this point, once he learns that he will get a bite only after he barks, you have the hold and bark complete with the 'out'.

The Drive

Introduce the drive when additional defence pressure is necessary. In the beginning, the drive is simply moving the dog whilst on the sleeve with collar pressure from the back-tie or long line. Once the dog is on the sleeve, the helper brings the sleeve close, forcing the dog to commit to the helper's body. The helper proceeds to drag the dog on the *non-sleeve* side. The helper's body must be turned sideways to avoid stepping on paws. Once the dog is familiar with driving, the helper strokes the dog's sides with his free hand. This prepares the dog for the added pressure of the padded stick.

The Stick

To keep the pressure off the dog, do not introduce the stick simultaneously with the drive. Stick use starts at the intermediate level of defence techniques whilst on the back-tie. Its introduction is simply holding it during the bite. If the bite is sound, then stroking with the stick is permitted. Looking for stress, the helper now strikes the back-tie. Gradually work up to a couple of light taps, while always looking out for avoidance behaviours.

If the dog looks good, after a few sessions of simply light stroking and hitting the back-tie or taut long line, strike him sharply and release the sleeve for the win. For the remainder of the session return to light stroking as though nothing had happened. Never strike sharply more than twice, and do not strike sharply during the next session. The objective is to teach the dog to endure the added defence pressure while remaining on the bite and under control. Once the dog has learned the drive and is familiar with the occasional two sharp strikes of the stick whilst on the sleeve, combine the drive with the stick.

The most common reason for stick shyness is its use as a weapon or 'training' device. The former occurs to threaten the dog, while the latter punishes the dog during conflict, for behaviour such as nipping during the hold and bark. If the dog

Stroking lightly with the stick.

Long line stick strike.

re-bites the sleeve or nips the helper (also known as being 'dirty'), the handler gives an immediate verbal correction and returns to the long line connected to the training collar. Competent handlers often use two long lines (one for each collar) to maintain training progress.

With the exception of *extreme* cases, do not use the stick to correct behaviour. A second stick mistake made by poor trainers is hitting sharply with every bite, or striking five or six times. This form of abuse is *not* training.

The Courage Test

Although it is not within the scope if this book to analyse every Schutzhund routine it is necessary to discuss the courage test, for this determines whether or not we have a protection dog. The courage test begins with the dog and handler separated by seventy paces. The decoy yells and aggressively charges the team. The handler then releases the dog who runs full speed toward the attacking decoy. Without slowing, the dog must grip the sleeve and stay on during the drive. At the end of the drive the dog must out on command. The difficulty of this test is the great distance away from the handler.

Once the dog performs consistently well in holds, releases and drives, it is time to combine these behaviours with distance from the handler. The following techniques build upon Schutzhund defensive test routines.

Begin the session by using the long line to do a few runaway bites with the handler jogging behind the dog. With the runaway warm-up, he is now ready for the double runaway. Increase the distance between the helper and dog. Still on the long line, the dog pursues the fleeing helper. The helper suddenly turns and runs toward the dog; simultaneously the handler releases the line. When the dog is about 10–15 ft (3–4.5 m) from the helper, the decoy again turns to give the dog a runaway bite.

Over several sessions, gradually replace the second runaway portion with a back-pedal. Facing the dog, the back-pedalling decoy applies reduced defensive pressure. Use this technique over many sessions, slowly reducing the number of backward paces from about twenty to ten. After several sessions of back-pedalling, slowly decrease the number of back-pedal steps until the helper backs up only a few feet.

Now the dog is ready for the training catch. After a couple of warm-up runaway bites, perform another runaway with the dog 5 ft (1.5 m) behind the decoy. The helper suddenly turns to face the dog, stops and places the sleeve in the high attack position with the bite bar facing down. The dog is pulling the handler on the long line a few feet away. When the helper turns, stops, and holds the sleeve high, the handler simultaneously releases the line and gives the 'bite' command. If the dog misses the sleeve, the handler takes up the slack while the helper runs off. The fleeing helper frustrates the dog and helps him to concentrate on the next bite.

The training catch requires a certain amount of practice on the part of the decoy. The dog is striking hard because of all the runaways and back-pedalling. The decoy must maintain the novice dog's strong strike by absorbing the sleeve impact. As the dog hits the sleeve, the good decoy must move the upper body and even the feet, if necessary, to allow the dog to remain in his path of momentum. Keeping the dog in the path of his momentum eliminates physical twisting that may cause injury and training setbacks. Just as the energy from the dog's flight path dissipates, the decoy must bend at the waist to allow all four of the dog's feet to contact the ground. From this point, depending upon the dog's level of experience, the decoy may drive, fight, or slip the sleeve.

With a successful bite, the dog essentially completes a mini-courage test with the training catch. Over several sessions, increase the release distance up to about seventy paces. Again, regardless of what stage the dog is at in training experience, the helper rarely does the full stop catch, but absorbs the crash by either pivoting and stepping in harmony with the dog's momentum, placing him lightly upon the ground, or by stepping backward two or three feet.

Dog approaching fast: note decoy's right leg ready to absorb impact by stepping back.

Dog hits sleeve, decoy begins to rock back.

Decoy moves the right leg further back to softly absorb dog's momentum.

The decoy places the novice dog safely on all fours.

The following is a slightly advanced exercise leading up to the courage test attack. The handler holds the dog as the helper agitates a *short* distance away. With the dog worked up in drive, the handler releases the dog with the 'bite' command, while the helper stays in one position, threatening the dog up to the bite. Work on both of these methods (runaway and stop, turn and bite and the above) either during the same session or every other session, depending upon the dog.

There are two types of trial catch: the front and the side. In the front catch, the helper runs toward the dog and slows when a few feet from him. The helper *must stop* just before the bite. After the stop, the helper turns roughly 180 degrees to their left and drives the dog. Competent trainers consider this method a safe trial procedure. Inexperienced helpers usually crash into the dog, producing quite a show, but this can also cause injuries or training difficulties for the dog.

The European side catch is more difficult for the young dog with targeting problems. It is very much similar to the frontal catch but, instead of stopping, the helper moves two or three steps to the side away from the sleeve. For the inexperienced helper, the problem with this catch is the possibility of incorrectly continuing to move forward once the dog grips the sleeve. The dog ends up gripping the sleeve over the helper's shoulder and hangs on as his body uses up momentum, similar to the cracking of a whip. The dog who hangs on goes for a nasty ride, while the dog who slips off hits the ground painfully. As with the incorrect front catch, this puts on quite a show and makes the helper look good, but the helper is not there for that purpose.

Once the dog has learned the courage test, knowledgeable trainers go back to drive development, working defence and some prey. The reason to avoid doing the test frequently is twofold: the risk of injury, and the tendency for the dog to slow before the bite. Avoidance may or may not be the reason for slowing. If you recall, the dog runs at top speed because of the work done leading up to the test. Remember all the running away? The dog expects the helper to run away. However, when they learn that the helper may stop, some dogs slow.

Remember to use drive development whether or not the need is apparent. The more negative and stressful the training process becomes, the more attitude work is necessary. Give the dog a break from working on the courage test, outing, holds and bark, etc., and provide prey or defence work with little pressure. Superior trainers such as Rose state emphatically that:

> It should not be assumed that the dog does not require further training in this area simply because it has advanced to other work. Work on bites and confidence will always be a factor in training, even after achieving Schutzhund III several times. Additionally, drive work removes some of the pressure resulting from other training.[5]

Prey move for the advanced dog.

[5]Rose 1985, page 217, et al.

SUMMARY

In summary, there are two basic bite drives or attitudes; prey and defence. The working protection dog must have a balance of both, the former for control and trainability (willingness) and the latter for 'hardness' or gameness. The truly game dog simply will not back down, and this is what honest people need in the face of a determined attacker. Therefore, the defence spirit is crucial.

There are several indicators that the dog is too high in defence for training purposes. A weak and chewy bite; backing off on the bite; avoiding the frontal position of the decoy; being easily distracted (smelling the grass, listening to birds or automobile horns, etc). If the predominantly defence dog is too high in defence, he becomes uncontrollable, refuses to follow commands, and the bite becomes frontal instead of full.

A common novice mistake is to advance the dog's training into defence before he is ready. Remember to make progress slowly, spending several weeks on teaching each new behaviour.

For advanced training procedures and techniques, please see the suggested reading list in the Bibliography. You will find there several works devoted to the advanced protection and control procedures necessary for passing Schutzhund tests.

CHAPTER FIVE

Tracking

Many experienced trainers often express the opinion that tracking is the most challenging area of training. It is certainly true that the well-fed tracking dog must learn to concentrate tenaciously for a long time. As is often the case, some young or under-trained dogs cannot continue the moment a noise disrupts concentration. However, these problems are easily overcome. Most trainers agree that teaching the dog the process of tracking should use good technique and begin at about five weeks of age.

We often hear that up to two years work is necessary to produce a reliable tracker. Yet the puppy is a natural tracker. At five weeks old, with some handler help, pups track thirty paces for bait, including a right-angled turn. Further, many pups, without help, turn about and track all the way back to the scent pad. To the amazement of many trainers, we often watch a pup at play discover the now obliterated track, several days old, follow it and find dried-up bait!

During the dog's first months of training, because progress may be slow, the handler must learn patience, being certain not to consider tracking mistakes or enthusiasm as disobedience. The need for patience extends especially to the tone of voice commands. Tracking commands and encouragement must be calm, regardless of handler frustrations or ego-driven expectations. During the track, the handler maintains calmness and concentration by softly using familiar phrases borrowed from obedience work such as 'that's it', or 'that's a good dog', to support the dog on the track. The beginner or novice tracking dog does not receive training collar or verbal corrections, since he will have virtually no understanding of what he did to deserve a correction. While there may be mild training collar corrections for the advanced tracker, the handler need not scold a dog verbally, regardless of experience.

Do not correct tracking enthusiasm.

With very little experience, pups learn from contextual clues what is expected. In this case, a fourteen-week-old pup tracking.

For example, for the inexperienced dog – one who is not sure of what he is doing – the handler merely gives a calm tracking command or finger assistance the moment the dog raises his nose off the track. Once the dog returns to the track, the handler again offers soft words of encouragement as though nothing happened. The reason for the raised nose may be unusual noises, change in tracking terrain, desiring eye contact with the handler or merely sight-seeing. By firmly but calmly asking the dog to continue tracking, the young tracker learns that he must concentrate on the track until the handler tells him otherwise.

On the other hand, when working an experienced tracker, he may need anything from a very mild to a firm training collar correction, combined with a stern tracking command, the very moment he raises his head to gaze at something over his shoulder. When he gets back to the track the handler once again gives soft words of encouragement as though nothing happened. The handler does not express any irritation in his voice or body language. Soon, the dog returns to working and forgets the correction, yet he learns that he may receive another correction if he stops tracking. Given the slow tracker, trainers who teach this method very well do not need a tracking line even during severely testing situations.

Pronounced verbal encouragement and food reinforcement (placed in the footsteps) aid the young dog in overcoming both internal and external obstacles. Physiologically, the dog must learn to scent the track whilst breathing. This is not essentially new to the dog, since he does it naturally. The only unusual aspect is that he must maintain concentration upon any command, and this is the source of tracking difficulty. Also, he must keep his nose close to the ground and deal with the clutter of scent that occurs with varying types of ground cover, insects and prey activity.

To teach the dog good tracking skills, we start with bait. In a way similar to tracking prey, baiting a track provides motivation. Since we already know that positive motivation is the method of choice in new learning situations, we see that this tracking method harmonizes with the pup's past experience, making the trainer's task a little easier.

Food Motivation

> When some hunter wishes to make trials of his dogs, he carries in his hands a hare, dead or alive, and walks forward in a devious path, now pursuing a straight course, now aslant, left or right twining his crooked way, but when he has come far from the gates of the city, he digs a trench and buries the hare. Returning to the city, he straightway brings near the path the cunning dog and immediately it is excited at the scent of the hare and seeks the track upon the ground. When at last he hits the airy trail, he gives tongue and whines with joy.
>
> Oppian, third century AD[1]

Despite the difficulty that some trainers may have in teaching tracking, Oppian reminds us that teaching the dog to track is by no means a new skill. It is probable that the use of food to teach tracking is older than his third-century observation. Cave wall paintings, some many thousands of years old, depict the wounded and fleeing bison with a dog and handler on its trail. It is possible that, pretty much as long as human beings have been hunting, the dog has been close by.

The choice of bait is left up to the handler's imagination. Diced

[1]Mahir 1970, page 3.

pieces of hotdogs, tiny balls of cheese, small bits of cooked hamburger, pieces of left over turkey and chicken; whatever the dog enjoys eating – which may be almost anything for dogs with high drives. What prudent trainers enjoy about tracking is that any meat or cheese left over from the table ends up in the refrigerator and eventually goes on the tracking field.

At the tracking field, the handler, with a plastic bag of small pieces of bait and a hungry dog on standby, takes a large step into the target area to create the scent pad. The scent pad is stamped into a triangular shape, with a 2 ft (0.6 m) base, pointing in the direction of the track. This relatively large area of disturbed ground will eventually give the young dog a clue as to the odour of the track. In order to teach the pup to search the scent pad thoroughly, many trainers stamp several pads, baiting each, but not making a connecting track. This method teaches the dog to concentrate first on the pad. Dogs not taught this scent pad method generally don't waste time on the pad, since they know from experience what is ahead. Pups with very high enthusiasm simply charge down the track without taking much scent at the pad. For some dogs, failing to take enough scent at the pad taxes their memory of what the track should smell like. For others, taking only a little scent at the pad is apparently sufficient, or else they simply figure it out from the footsteps themselves.

Place a marking flag on the left side of the scent pad so that you will easily find your track when you fetch the dog. Set several small pieces of bait on the pad. Searching for the bait forces the dog to take up the track scent. Start your track by pounding hard, much as a marching soldier, with steps close together, baiting each step. Do this by taking a step, lifting the heel and placing the bait. Alternatively, place a piece of bait underneath a boot toe. Another modification is to slide your boot back slightly and place the bait in the now larger and easier to follow footprint. As the dog catches on to tracking, mix the various forms of bait placement and frequency. For example, after baiting each toe of a footstep for the first sessions, begin to bait the heel portion. Change reward frequency by failing to bait a step every so often. As the dog gains experience, continue to reduce bait frequency, especially with easy tracking conditions of a freshly disc-harrowed field. You'll be bending over a lot with a beginner dog! Later in this chapter, we will return to the subject of baiting.

For the very young or beginner dog, start with fifteen-pace tracks, slowly working up to seventy paces. Many new handlers ask when to start turns. Since, at five weeks old, our puppies do turns in a 15 ft (4.5 m) track, we advocate teaching turns with the first finger track in the house and continue when outside (see Chapter 2).

Finger help.

When you decide that the track is long enough, jump out of it just as you jumped into the scent pad, and remember where it ends. At first, the completed beginner track resembles a trench, in that the steps are deep and close together so that the track's end is readily apparent. Do not use a flag to mark the end, as this may eventually cause training problems with the dog, for he will associate the track's end with the flag and refuse to track past it. For advanced tracking you will need to use flags to mark turns to determine whether the dog is on track, therefore use a natural item to mark the end. When the dog reaches the end of the track, begin a play routine with physical and verbal enthusiasm. Some trainers place a small pile of bait at the end. In no time, the pup learns whatever signal you teach to stop tracking.

For training purposes, try to use a disced field (some erroneously consider this 'ploughed'). Disced earth is fairly flat and soft; it shows tracks clearly and has less distracting smells than those found in a grass field. In the beginning, it is important to see your track so that you can help the novice dog when he makes a mistake.

Discing equipment on a disced field.

Trench track on a clean disced field.

Alternatively, beginner dogs may also use the more difficult grassy field. We have often used the relatively short, mown lawn grass in backyards and public parks. In this case, track in the early hours, since the morning dew helps the handler to locate the track.

Depending upon the age and personality of the dog, you can track with anything from a training collar to a harness. Be ready to change tracking gear depending upon the dog's comfort and performance. We started tracking a high-spirited Doberman at one and a half years old with a pinch collar. He had no problem with the collar for several months, and gained confidence. However, increased confidence soon translated into harder pulling. This caused several problems. Since he felt confident with what was required, which was for him to find the track and the articles, any pinch collar constriction resulting from his hard pulling produced even harder pulling, because he thought he was being corrected for not tracking. Furthermore, the harder he pulled, the more difficulty he had with breathing. When switched to a harness, he breathed easier and appeared comfortable, yet still pulled like a tractor. At first, if he needed a correction, we simply took the pinch collar lead that dragged underneath him. Eventually, we removed the training collar entirely since he was doing so well. For years he tracked just fine with only the harness. Then, at just over five years of age, he began to take tracking less seriously, so we simply placed the training collar in its familiar position. Without any corrections, that dog got serious.

Beside the tracking harness, there is one other trial option; the fur-saver collar. Since a slow and methodical tracker is not pulling the lead hard enough to cause a breathing problem, the fur-saver is adequate on the dead ring. This is a choke chain with extra large rings, designed not to pull hair. For training purposes, whether the handler uses a leather collar, pinch collar, fur-saver or the tracking harness, it is the dog's tracking behaviour and level of tracking experience that determine selection. The handler must evaluate the dog and use the equipment that suits, and be willing to change it according to circumstances.

While beginning training, the handler must stay either next to the dog or directly behind him. With either of these two positions, the handler can use the 6 ft (1.8 m) leash connected to the harness or collar effectively. With progress, start using the 30 ft (9 m) line, but still remain directly behind the dog initially, dragging the remaining line.

After several sessions of using specialized tracking equipment (for example, perhaps a harness and the long line), the dog knows exactly what work is at hand the moment the handler reaches for the gear. Another benefit of using the long line during training is that distance between the team becomes flexible. In easier sections of the track, line should be released to increase the distance between handler and dog. This will let the dog become familiar with working independently from the handler. Conversely, in difficult sections, the handler should be next to the dog, ready to help. Regardless of the distance from the dog, the handler should keep providing verbal encouragement if the dog is on task.

In a trial, the handler will walk 30 ft (9 m) behind the tracking dog. The purpose of a 30 ft (9 m) tracking long line is twofold. First, although a trained dog will track without line, some dogs have a speed problem. The long line keeps the dog from going too fast and overshooting both turns and articles. Second, the 30 ft (9 m) distance between the handler and the experienced tracking dog is ideal for keeping the handler out of the dog's way. If the dog does overshoot a turn, the handler is far enough back so as not to foul the track and thereby confuse the dog.

Novice handlers often ask when to begin putting distance between themselves and the dog. Throughout training, the primary position for the handler is directly behind the tracking dog. This is true no matter how good the dog becomes. However, as mentioned earlier, you should increase the working distance slowly when the dog tracks easy sections. It is helpful if you leave an article at the completion of a relatively easy section (more on articles later). Thus, when you tackle the track, allow the dog distance on the easy section and catch up when he 'downs' on the article before a difficult segment. With advanced dogs, intermittently allow the dog to track the whole distance using the entire length of line.

Going back to our freshly laid track, get your dog ready by first allowing him to relieve himself at a distance. With your equipment secure, and you at his side or slightly behind him, walk to the pad and softly give the 'track' command. If he does not yet know the track command or needs help with the pad or the next footprint, immediately lean over and point out the bait while simultaneously giving the command. By 'pointing' at the bait, we mean that you may have to touch the bait if he needs that amount of help. For the novice dog, no matter what the subject, always err on the side of too much help, rather than not enough.

At first, the pup will search diligently for each piece of bait. However, for the very young, experience may be detrimental in that enthusiasm gets the upper hand. The high-drive pup will switch to sight tracking and plough right over every piece of bait except for the larger pieces. In this event, go back to finger tracking. By pointing out each small piece of bait, while gently slowing his progress with the line, he will learn again to use his nose. It is important that he learns early on to search each footprint for bait. Soon, the young pup will move his head from side-to-side, searching the entire width of the track.

Over several sessions of short tracks with each footstep close together and baited, begin randomly to leave a step without bait. Gradually, you should experiment between heavy baiting and no baiting (for example, bait five consecutive steps and then leave five steps without bait) while carefully watching the tracking dog for signs of motivational difficulty. Signs of difficulty range from refusal to track forward, lifting the head and looking around, or looking to the handler for help. If the pup lacks motivation to track on lightly baited tracks, go back in training and bait more heavily for a few sessions.

If you elect not to teach turns from the beginning, as many trainers advocate, then be aware that you may be teaching the dog that tracks are always straight, and this is contrary to what we are trying to do. The myth that young dogs must start on straight tracks may be the source of some trainers' tracking problems.

Start right-angle turns by triple laying. This means pack your steps during the turn, go on for a few feet, turn about and follow your own track through the turn; then turn about for the second time and follow your track though the turn, but this time baiting each step. Work on turns in combination with the straight track. As the dog becomes accustomed to changes of direction, stop triple laying and gradually reduce baiting the turns. You must be ready to provide finger assistance the moment the dog becomes obviously confused.

A word about 'confusion' may be necessary. If the novice-advanced dog misses a turn or goes off the track for a few feet, but catches himself, no correction may be necessary since wind may have pushed the entire scent of the next tracking leg in the wrong direction. In the case of the really experienced advanced dog, it is best to correct mildly using the training collar the moment you are certain that he has drifted off the track or missed a turn. The reason for the correction is that his concentration may be wandering.

Tracking Corrections

Corrections will be necessary eventually, but should be muted. Using corrections of the type normally reserved for obedience has no place on the novice track and serves only to confuse the young dog. When the handler feels that a strong correction may be necessary, we see pressure to progress too fast. Strong corrections in tracking cause confusion, which counters what we are doing, that is, building confidence and concentration. Remember, dogs are born with the fundamentals of tracking. Therefore, we are not trying to teach tracking, but are merely teaching the dog to track what we want upon command.

Nevertheless, dogs come in varying personalities, therefore strong compulsion may be necessary for the more experienced trackers. Konrad Most claims:

> Compulsion, in a stronger or weaker form, will be found essential with many dogs if good service in tracking is to be obtained from them. It is not only a question of achieving the exclusive use of the nose. The inclination to track can itself be increased by properly applied compulsion once the dog has arrived at a stage when he is aware that he can at once escape compulsion by the use of the nose. As training proceeds, compulsion must also be applied whenever the dog yields to other inclinations, if he sniffs at a mouse hole,

for instance. The severity of the correction may be increased proportionately as the dog's ability to track improves. The encouragement given when an object is found must, however, be all the stronger, so that the animal's pleasure in the work may be constantly renewed and intensified.[2]

Articles

The novice dog now tracks 400 paces (in a disced field) and has little difficulty with turns. At this level of experience, when working an easy track, the handler may use mild corrections. Now is the time to start work with articles. Articles such as a glove, wallet, or anything with human scent, are dropped directly on the track by the track layer. The dog must indicate that he scents these items by downing, sitting or standing upon them. Some trainers ask the dog to pick up the articles and retrieve.

The dog identifies, and is taught to lie down on articles, not because they are a part of the track scent, but because they have human scent. After a few minutes of ageing, the track itself has little or no human scent. The tracking dog follows the scent of crushed vegetation or soil left by the track layer's boot. Each footprint leaves scent evidence of various crushed living and inorganic material, which provides scent discrimination from the scent outside the print. Since the track itself has very little human scent, and the articles have a lot of human scent, then we may introduce 'downing' upon articles off the track and incorporate them into the track later.

If we teach indicating articles away from the track, then we should do it during obedience training. After all, this is an obedience task. Lay a few personal items with your scent on them on the ground in a straight line. (If they are not already scented, place them against your skin for a few minutes.) With the dog at heel, walk him toward the first article, point to it, and give a mild downward pop with the training collar, placing him in the 'down' position. When he lies down, make a big scene over how good he was to do so on the article. Pick up the article, let him smell it, get

[2]Most 1955, pages 196, 208.

excited and provide reinforcement. He won't have a clue as to what you're doing, but do this down the line of articles. That is, position the dog in a 'down' using a pop of the training collar (without command), playing, and allowing him to smell each article. (If you command the dog to lie down and then pop him with the collar, you are merely reinforcing compliance to your verbal command.) When you do this for a few minutes every day, he will soon begin to lie down on his own.

When he lies down on the articles consistently, introduce an article on the track. Whilst on the track, if you see him smell the article and he does not down, give a 'down' correction and point to the article. Since he knows that he is to lie down on the article, go ahead and also use the verbal 'down' command when on the track. However, if you believe that he did not smell the article, then it is best not to correct. It is possible he missed the article on an exhalation, thereby making any correction a possible source of confusion. Of course, when he first downs on his own, make a fuss of his new behaviour exactly as you did during article training.

As the dog progresses on a track containing articles, problems will arise. Sometimes the dog will lie down a few feet in front of the article, or he may cover it with his body. There is a little magic trick that often helps get the dog to lie down with the article between his front legs. The first step is to place a piece of bait under the article. This will keep him close and not lying on top of it. Be sure to correct him into a down on the article if he's more concerned about standing over it to eat the bait – which typically happens the first few times using this method. After a few sessions stop baiting articles and do the following. With bait ready in your right hand, watch the dog as he lies down on an unbaited article. Approach and lift the article, putting your right hand under it while simultaneously exposing the bait. This sleight-of-hand trick will condition the dog to associate the article with bait, but without him mouthing or playing with the article (which will eventually occur with article baiting, thereby causing a loss of concentration). This conditioning works even if the dog knows where the bait is coming from. Continue further work on the article routine during obedience training.

If a dog lies down about 25 ft (8 m) away from the article on the upwind leg, and you have tried the methods of correction above, then give a mild pop with the training collar in the direction of the track. The confusion here is that the dog believes he must lie down when he smells the article, whereas we are teaching the dog to both smell and find the article by following the track.

The more tracking the dog does, the better the result. As the dog gets better and does a 400 pace track with turns and articles, use different fields with various levels of difficulty as defined by difficulty in seeing footprints. A track is too hard when the dog needs a lot of help. Quartering back and forth over the track and lack of concentration are also indicators of a difficult track. When laying a track in bad tracking conditions, or with cover changes, step harder, use more bait, and make it short. Don't forget to help the dog by pointing out the track, if necessary.

While we're on the topic of cover changes, let's consider hard surface tracking. It is possible to track on hard surfaces given the correct conditions. An experienced trainer points out that:

> Until quite recently it was not thought possible that dogs could track with any degree of success or accuracy over hard surfaces, and it has been necessary to develop new and better training techniques to ensure that the dog is given every assistance. Perhaps the most important of these new techniques...has been the instruction of the handlers in such a way that they are well versed in the theories of scent, able to appraise the value of the existing weather conditions and to read the reactions of the dog intelligently.[3]

Once the handler understands basic dog learning theory, works the dog often enough to gain experience and applies teaching techniques and expectations that fit the dog, a team exists. This is so because only the experienced handler can read the dog with nearly 100 per cent accuracy. The handler reaches this level of effectiveness by tracking often and over many conditions and ground covers, and by paying close attention to the dog, noting the causes of each particular body expression. Each dog has his own way of showing feelings whilst on the track. The handler must create a tenable

[3]Mahir 1970, page 85.

theory for each feeling the dog expresses and must compare the body language with past instances to test the theory for confirmation or alteration. With enough handler and dog tracking experience, tracking a person through some of the most difficult terrain becomes possible.

Tracking Conditions

Ageing and weather conditions cause deterioration of track scent. With age, each footprint's scent becomes similar to the surrounding cover. It is important to note that weather influences the process of track deterioration to varying degrees. As a rule, conditions are good with moisture and no wind. For instance, our freshly disced field is moist and excellent for tracking.[4] Higher air than ground temperature helps tracking conditions. The cooler ground tends to pull heat and scent into the track. On the other hand, when the ground temperature is higher than that of the air, rising heat dissipates scent. Further, scent dissipation accelerates in dryness, low humidity, heat and strong winds.

Along with these general guidelines, there are individual tracking characteristics that are important to consider, especially for police handlers. Concrete, asphalt and stone surfaces need moisture or still water. Stone surfaces cannot be jagged; smoother is easier for the dog. In hot conditions, asphalt irritates a dog's nose even if it is wet. Asphalt irritation also occurs in cooler, drier conditions, but to a lesser extent.

Remember that conditions associated with heat apply to sand. Dogs find loose, wet sand easier to scent than that which is packed and dry. Also, the less sunlight, the better tracking conditions will be. Furthermore, tracks laid after dark will last in fresh condition until morning: this is true for most tracking conditions.

Snow, frost and early morning dew provide tracking conditions similar to disced field tracking, making these conditions ideal for learning. Snow-covered tracks are still trackable up to about 2 in

[4]'Moisture' includes ice, frost and snow.

(5 cm) in depth. However, melting snow makes tracking difficult in run-off conditions.

High humidity and rain with no run-off provide great conditions for tracking. (Keep in mind that search dogs easily scent drowned bodies in quiet and fairly deep lake water. Curiously, water is a good scent conductor.) Again, for training or testing, the early morning dew makes the driest ground trackable.

Wind direction may confuse the young tracker by masking turns or pushing him off the centre of the track (see Novice Tracking Problems, page 146). Usually bait will pull the tracker back on line. Tracking experience overcomes most wind problems, but the handler must make a wind estimation before tracking, if only to predict problems.

Cross-tracks

Dogs must have instruction to stay on one track. When the dog does take a cross-track, it may not be because he didn't notice the new scent; it may be that the handler simply did not teach him to stay on the original track. Cross-track training is not difficult, but takes practice.

During training, as you approach a cross-track, look for a physical reaction from the dog. For instance, if the dog doesn't immediately take the cross-track, he may turn his nose slightly in its direction as he continues past. When the dog does take the cross-track, gently slow his progress with the leash and point with your hand at the bait on the correct track (bait past the intersection – see illustration page 146). By no means correct the dog who takes the cross-track as this is contrary to the principle of tracking. That is, correcting the dog may be teaching him not to track.

When teaching the dog to deal with cross-tracks, be certain to bait the correct track two or three steps on the other side of the cross-track. At this point, confusion may set upon the dog since he believes that he is being taught not to turn, because when he scents a turn (in this case the incorrect cross-track) all he has to do is to go

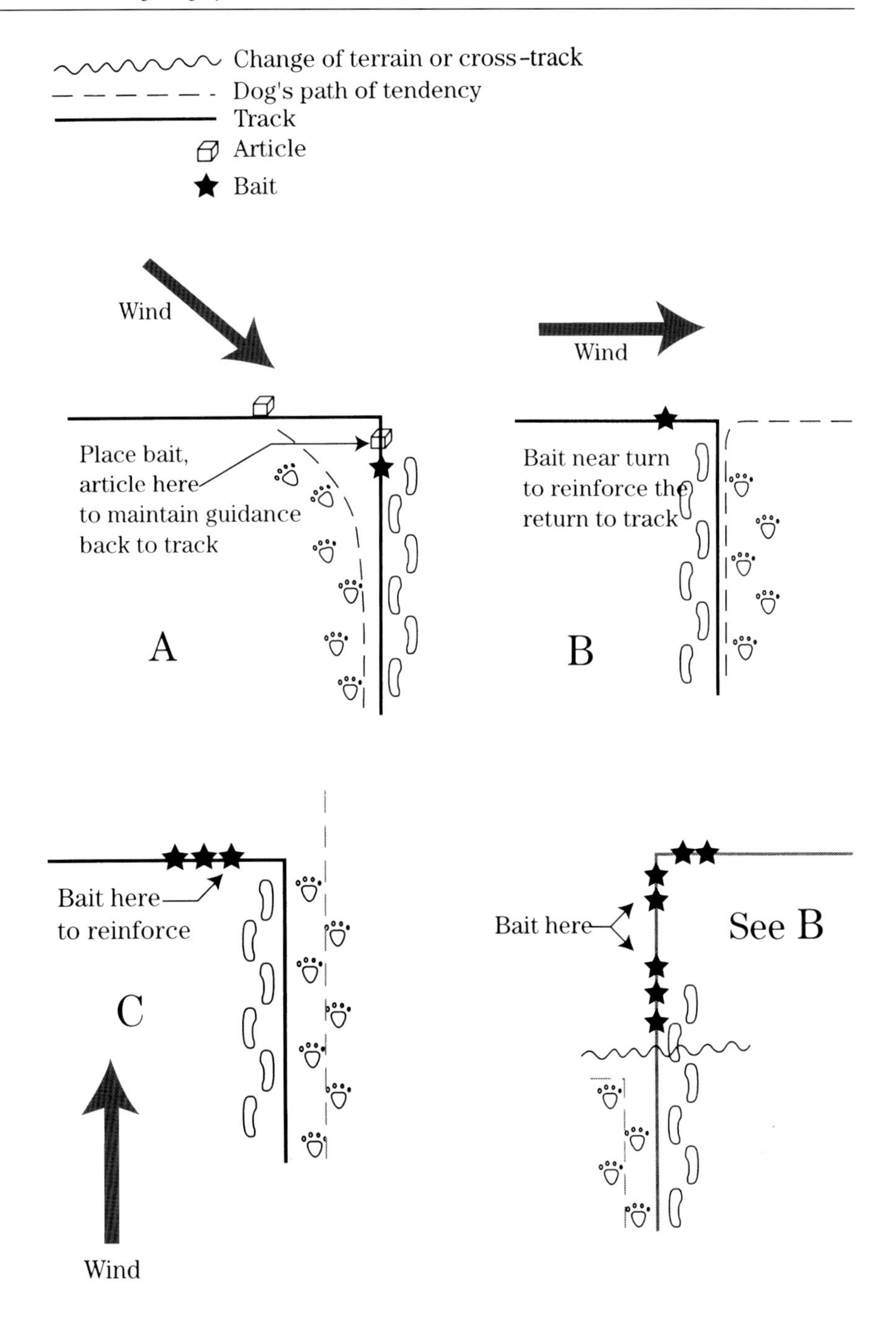

Novice tracking problems

straight and find a track with bait. Therefore, it is important to take a few steps backward in training and again bait the correct turns when teaching cross-tracks. After a while, he will begin to discriminate between the older and fresher tracks, assuming that you work with cross-tracks that are at least a day old.

Konrad Most makes an important point about the track-sure dog and articles which is useful for the new handler, especially the new police officer handler.

> Dogs trained not to switch between older and later tracks may be called track-sure dogs. No doubt the variations of scent caused by the time differences have something to do with it. The track-sure dog is exclusively concerned with human tracks and takes note of objects lying on the track only if they bear human scent. It does not necessarily follow, however, in such cases, that the objects indicated have been in contact with the person providing the track.[5]

Do not lay your track, then immediately lay your cross-track! The dog will correctly make no distinction between the tracks because there is none. However, you may use the previous day's track for a cross-track because of differences in ageing. Alternatively, you may have a second person of different physical size from the original track layer to lay the cross-track.

The ultimate difficult cross-track is a road. Avoid teaching the dog to track proficiently on a road, but teach that the track will continue on the other side. Do this during training by leading him across and baiting the track heavily on the far side. The dog learns that when a road masks his track, it will continue on the other side.

In the case of the track-sure dog, the age of the track is a significant factor in scenting. Johnson conducted several experiments on cross-tracks that tend to show a weakness in even the track-sure dog:

> The experiments I conducted with two different track layers on the 'X' pattern showed that the dog could in fact tell the difference between two tracks that were laid by two different track layers as long as there was a great weight differential on tracks over two hours in age. Should the weight of the

[5]Most 1955, page 177.

> two track layers be equal then the dogs could tell the difference between the two tracks when fresh, but not when they were over two hours old.[6]

The X pattern referred to is laid by two people. One person lays the right half of the X, essentially a sideways V track, and the other track layer completes the X pattern. The middle of the X, of course, contains two possibilities for the dog: turn or go straight. The highly trained tracker makes a distinction between track layers of identical weight until the tracks are about two hours old. This distinction comes from different soles of the shoe or boot that help distinguish the track from others. It is not the sole of the shoe that is scented, but its particular pattern that creates a special scent when mashing the ground. But, after two hours, the weathering effect takes its toll, making the track indistinguishable from others laid at the same time by a person of about the same weight.

Following a track laid by someone else should not be a problem. The dog will follow the track exactly as taught since, with ageing, personal scent is not important, just the disturbed ground. Yet there may be some difficulty when it comes to the weight of the track layer and walking style. The smaller the track layer, the less ground each footprint disturbs; further, the taller the track layer, the more distance between footprints. Both may foul tracking concentration for the novice dog. Therefore, when preparing your dog to follow the track of others, vary your own track during practice as much a possible.

Like other aspects of training, teaching the tracking dog is an art-form based upon close and reflective observation of the dog. Dog training is not an exact science. With each displayed behaviour, there are reinforcers or corrections. For the competent handler and trainer, the dog 'teaches' the trainer how to proceed. When the dog has difficulty, it is up to the handler to use available resources, such as experience, intelligence, and when all else fails, imagination! Your dog may demand a plan of action that is completely novel and never tried.

[6]Johnson 1975, page 149.

SUMMARY

In summary, begin teaching the very young pup to track, using close footsteps (trenching). If necessary, go over the track three times while baiting heavily on the last pass. Teach right-angle turns from the very beginning. Whenever the dog appears confused, be certain to help by pointing out the bait with a finger while simultaneously using the track command. In rough sections of the track, remember to bait heavily and stomp hard. Remember to drone soft verbal reinforcement when the dog is on track.

Teach indicating articles off the track, making it an obedience routine. Only combine the two behaviours when both are going well and you are able to predict success.

At the advanced stages, keep in mind how weather may influence tracking conditions. In general, the more moist and humid tracking conditions are, the greater the likelihood of an easy track.

Imtroducing the 'stay'.

Conclusion

Whatever the training goal, it must proceed from a foundation of respect for the working dog. A brief survey of dictionaries shows that the word 'respect' has several definitions, yet they have one definitive term in common: 'consideration'. The working dog handler must show sincere consideration for the dog. The only way to show this is to view the world through the eyes of the dog, and this begins with the very young pup. Without the use of corrections, the pup learns the basics of tracking, obedience and rag work. If there are no corrections, the pup remains happy and looks forward to training sessions throughout life. The handler who refrains from working with the very young pup, because of a desire for 'the pup to be a pup', not only fails to utilize a period of the pup's life when imprinting for later training is optimal, but also limits the pup's potential. With structured daily training, the twenty-week-old already knows tracking fundamentals, bites a rag with enthusiasm and shows basic obedience behaviours. All such behaviour is important, no matter how baby-like. This basis of knowledge sets the stage for the more serious work that comes later, for the pup will happily apply the preliminary teaching that used play and food rewards to new training situations.

Lack of consideration for the dog produces emotional baggage that sabotages the team. Whilst handler anger and frustration result in confusion and over-correction, misguided devotion limits potential in the pup and is associated with a lack of correction, or under-correction, in the adult. The former occurs because the handler fails to exercise self-control; the latter because the handler believes that the working dog lacks, among other things, the intelligence to learn.

Respect for the working dog continues throughout training and training continues, in varying degrees, throughout life. The good handler learns to view the world from the dog's psychological orientation for as long as the team is together. Therefore, owning and training a working dog is a serious commitment.

APPENDIX

Recognized Working Titles

Titles awarded by USA Judges and Internationally recognized

SchHA	Introduction to Schutzhund work without tracking.
B	(Also BH) Basic companion dog.
AD	Endurance test for fundamental fitness.
WH	Watch Dog test for basic alertness.
SchH1	Preliminary Schutzhund qualification in tracking, obedience and protection.
SchH2	More challenging Schutzhund work in tracking, obedience and protection.
SchH3	Competition and Masters level of the three phases of Schutzhund.
FH1	Advanced tracking.
FH2	Greater tracking challenges.(Article placement determined by judge.)
IPO1	International trial, rules similar to the Schutzhund test but with some variations.
IPO2	More challenging Schutzhund work in tracking, obedience and protection.
IPO3	The competition level of IPO.

Additional SV Titles recognized by USA

BpDH1,2	Railway Police Dog
B1H	Blind Leader Dog
DH	Service Dog
DPH	Service Police Dog

FH	Tracking Dog (Same as USA)
HGH	Herding Dog
IPO1,2,3	International Rules (Same as USA)
LwH	Avalanche Dog
PFP1,2	Police Tracking Dog
PH	Police Dog
PSP1,2,3	Police Guard Dog
RtH	Rescue Dog
SchH1,2,3	Schutzhund titles (Same as USA)
ZFH	Customs Tracking Dog
ZH1,2,3	Customs Dog

USA recognized working titles from other countries

Africa	1WT 1,2,3
Austria	SchH1,2,3 and FHA 1,2,3
Belgium	Cereco1, 1WR1,2,3 equivalent to international IPO1,2,3
Czech Rep	ZVV1,2,3 equivalent to USA SchH1,2,3
Denmark	BHP1,2,3 equivalent to SchH1,2,3 and SPH equivalent to FH
England	PD
Finland	SK1 equivalent to IPO1
Holland	VH1,2,3 equivalent to SchH1,2 3 and SPH equivalent to FH
Italy	Brevetto 1,2,3 equivalent to SchH1,2,3
Poland	ZVV1,2,3 equivalent to SchH1,2,3
Switzerland	SchH, SchH B, SchH C, CHD1 equivalent to SchH1
Yugoslavia	CAB1,2,3 equivalent to SchH1,2,3

The information in this appendix is reproduced from *Schutzhund*, Vol. 22, No. 6, November/December 1997, p. 88 with the permission of the United Schutzhund Clubs of America.

Bibliography

Barwig, Susan, *The German Shepherd Book,* (Hoflin Publishing Ltd., Wheat Ridge, Colorado 1986).

Barwig, Susan & Stewart Hilliard, *Schutzhund Theory and Training Methods,* (Howell Book House, New York 1991).

Britford, D., *USAF Military Working Dog (MWD) Program,* (Department of the Air Force, USA 1980).

Fox, Michael W., *Superdog: Raising the Perfect Canine,* (Howell Book House, New York 1990).

Concepts In Ethology: Animal and Human Behavior (University of Minnesota, USA 1974).

Understanding Your Dog, (Coward, McCann & Geoghegan Inc., New York 1972).

Gray, Ernest A., *Dogs of War,* (Robert Hale, London 1989).

HM Government's Standing Advisory Committee on Police Dogs, *Police Dogs; Training and Care* (HMSO, London 1973).

Humphrey, Elliott & Lucien Warner, *Working Dogs,* (The John Hopkins Press, Baltimore 1934).

Jager, Theo. F., *Scout, Red Cross and Army Dogs,* (Arrow Printing Company, New York 1917).

Johnson, Glen R., *Tracking Dog Theory & Methods,* (Arner Publications Inc., Westmoreland, New York 1975).

Little, Brown, *The Monks of New Skete, How to Be Your Dog's Best Friend,* (Little, Brown and Company, Boston 1978).

MacInnes, John Watson, *Training Guard Dogs,* (A.S. Barnes and Company, New York 1955).

Mahir, Tom, *Police Dogs At Work,* (J.M. Dent & Sons Ltd., London 1970).

Most, Colonel Konrad, *Training Dogs,* (Coward-McCann Inc., New York 1955).

Patterson, Gary, *Schutzhund Protection Training,* (Sirius Publishing Company, Englewood, Colorado 1989).

Pearsall, Margaret E., *The Pearsall Guide to Successful Dog Training,* (Howell Book House Inc., New York 1974).

Pfaffenberger, Clarence, *The New Knowledge of Dog Behavior,* (Howell Book House Inc., New York 1984).

Pryor, Karen, *Lads Before the Wind,* (Sunshine Books, North Bend, Washington 1975).

Rapp, Jay, *How to Train Dogs for Police Work,* (Denlinger's Publishers Ltd., Fairfax, Virginia 1979).

Richardson, E.H., *British War Dogs,* (Skeffington & Son Ltd., London, 1920).

Rose, Tom & Gary Patterson, *Training the Competitive Working Dog,* (Giblaut Publishing Company, Englewood, Colorado 1985).

Scott, Tom, *Obedience and Security Training for Dogs* (Arco Publishing Company Inc., New York 1967).

Stephanitz, Max Von, *Schooling and Training the Shepherd Dog,* (Shepherd Dog Club of America Inc., New York 1922).

Varner, John Grier & Jeannette Johnson Varner, *Dogs of the Conquest,* (University of Oklahoma Press, USA 1983).

Wimhurst, C.G.E., *The Book of Working Dogs* (Frederick Muller Ltd., London 1967).

Index

Page numbers in *italics* refer to illustrations